Jorda

Everything You Need to Know

Introduction to Jordan: A Land of History and Diversity

In the heart of the Middle East, nestled within a region rich with history, culture, and natural wonders, lies the captivating country of Jordan. This land, steeped in the annals of time, offers a mesmerizing blend of history and diversity that beckons to travelers and explorers from around the world.

Jordan's geographical location is both a testament to its significance in history and a testament to its enduring appeal. It is strategically situated at the crossroads of Asia, Africa, and Europe, making it a vital point of convergence for ancient trade routes and civilizations. The country shares borders with Saudi Arabia to the south and southeast, Iraq to the northeast, Syria to the north, Israel and Palestine to the west, and the Red Sea to the southwest. Its varied terrain ranges from the arid deserts of Wadi Rum to the lush valleys of the Jordan River, providing a diverse landscape that mirrors its rich cultural tapestry.

To delve into Jordan's history is to embark on a journey through millennia. This land has been inhabited by humans for over 10,000 years, with evidence of ancient settlements dating back to the Paleolithic era. Archaeological sites such as 'Ain Ghazal reveal the existence of early agricultural communities. As history unfolded, Jordan became a cradle of civilization, witnessing the rise and fall of numerous empires and cultures.

One of the most iconic symbols of Jordan's historical legacy is the ancient city of Petra, often referred to as the "Rose-Red City." Carved into the rose-red cliffs of southern Jordan by the Nabateans more than 2,000 years ago, Petra stands as a testament to human ingenuity and architectural prowess. This UNESCO World Heritage site boasts a stunning array of rock-cut tombs, temples, and dwellings that tell the story of a thriving ancient civilization.

Throughout the ages, Jordan has played a pivotal role in the annals of history. The region was an integral part of the ancient kingdoms of Ammon, Moab, and Edom. Its terrain bore witness to the passage of legendary figures like Moses, whose journey through the desert of Wadi Musa is etched into biblical lore. The Roman Empire left its indelible mark on Jordan, with cities like Jerash showcasing the grandeur of Roman architecture and culture.

In the medieval era, Jordan became a focal point during the Crusades, with fortresses like Karak Castle bearing testament to the struggles for control over this prized land. The Ottoman Empire later ruled over Jordan for centuries, leaving behind a legacy that is still evident in the country's architecture and traditions.

The 20th century brought profound changes to Jordan's political landscape. It emerged as a modern nation under the leadership of King Abdullah I, marking the beginning of the Hashemite dynasty's rule. Since then, Jordan has stood as a beacon of stability and moderation in a region often marked by turmoil.

Today, Jordan remains a captivating blend of the ancient and the contemporary. Its vibrant cities like Amman offer a glimpse into modern Arab life, while its historical sites transport visitors back in time. The warmth and hospitality of its people, known as Jordanians, make every traveler feel like a welcomed guest.

Geographical Overview: Exploring Jordan's Varied Terrain

Nestled in the heart of the Middle East, Jordan boasts a geographical tapestry that is as diverse as it is enchanting. This ancient land is a living testament to the wonders of nature, with its terrain ranging from stark deserts to fertile valleys and rugged mountains.

One of the most iconic features of Jordan's landscape is the vast expanse of desert that stretches across its southern regions. The Wadi Rum desert, also known as the Valley of the Moon, is a mesmerizing sea of sand dunes and towering sandstone cliffs. It has a timeless, otherworldly quality that has captured the imagination of travelers and filmmakers alike. This area's unique topography has been shaped by wind and water over countless eons, creating a surreal and hauntingly beautiful landscape that seems straight out of a science fiction novel.

Moving eastward, the landscape undergoes a dramatic transformation as it gives way to the arid plains of the Badia region. Here, vast expanses of desert terrain are interspersed with patches of hardy vegetation that eke out an existence in this harsh environment. It's a place where the vastness of the desert truly comes to life, and where Bedouin nomads have roamed for generations.

In contrast, the fertile Jordan Valley, formed by the Jordan River, provides a lush and green corridor in the otherwise arid landscape. This valley is not only agriculturally rich but also holds tremendous historical and cultural significance. It is home to the ancient city of Jericho, one of the oldest continuously inhabited cities in the world, and has been a focal point for various civilizations throughout history.

To the west of the country, the Jordanian landscape transitions into the rolling hills and highlands that culminate in the capital city, Amman. These areas are known for their olive groves, vineyards, and agricultural terraces that have sustained communities for centuries. It's a testament to the resilience and resourcefulness of the people of Jordan, who have managed to cultivate the land and create pockets of greenery in an otherwise arid region.

The northern part of Jordan is dominated by the sprawling plateau of Al-Jazeera, which means "the island" in Arabic. This elevated region features a milder climate than the desert areas and is characterized by its fertile soil. The town of Ajloun, located here, is known for its lush forests and the imposing Ajloun Castle, offering a glimpse into the historical significance of this region.

And then there are the majestic mountains of Jordan. To the west, the mountains of the Dead Sea Rift rise dramatically, forming a natural barrier between Jordan and Israel. These rugged peaks are home to hidden valleys and pristine landscapes, where nature's beauty is on full display.

Jordan's geography is further enriched by its access to the Red Sea in the south, offering opportunities for marine exploration and tourism. The coastal city of Aqaba has become a bustling hub for those seeking the allure of both desert and sea.

Ancient Jordan: Tracing the Origins of Civilization

Archaeological excavations have revealed that humans have called this region home for over 10,000 years. These early inhabitants were nomadic hunter-gatherers, wandering through the fertile landscapes of the Jordan Valley and beyond. Their existence is documented through the discovery of ancient tools and primitive artifacts, scattered like breadcrumbs from the distant past.

The Neolithic era marked a significant turning point. It was during this period that the people of Jordan transitioned from nomadic lifestyles to settled communities. Agriculture and animal husbandry became the foundation of their livelihoods. Notably, 'Ain Ghazal, located near present-day Amman, stands as a testament to this era. Here, archaeologists have uncovered one of the world's oldest known villages, complete with remarkable plaster statues and structures that provide a glimpse into the burgeoning culture of this time.

Around 3,000 BCE, the Bronze Age brought about further evolution. Jordan became a crossroads for trade and cultural exchange, connecting the dots between Mesopotamia, Egypt, and the Mediterranean world. Emerging city-states, such as Umm el-Jimal and Bab edh-Dhra, thrived amidst the harsh desert surroundings.

As the Iron Age dawned, powerful kingdoms emerged on Jordanian soil. The kingdoms of Ammon, Moab, and Edom, among others, left an indelible mark with their impressive fortresses and temples. The Ammonites, in particular, crafted the formidable Amman Citadel, a testament to their architectural prowess and regional influence.

The rock-carved city of Petra, dating back to the 4th century BCE and founded by the Nabateans, is a jewel in Jordan's archaeological crown. This ancient marvel served as a bustling trading hub and a center of cultural exchange. Its iconic facades and intricate water management systems bear witness to the Nabateans' ingenuity.

The Roman Empire's conquest of Jordan in the 1st century CE ushered in a new era of cultural fusion. Roman cities like Jerash and Philadelphia (modern-day Amman) thrived, boasting grand temples, theaters, and public structures. These urban centers became vital hubs of commerce and cultural interchange.

As the sands of time continued to shift, so did the course of history in Jordan. The Byzantine and early Islamic periods left their marks on the landscape and culture. The Umayyad Desert Castles, scattered throughout the desert, are enduring examples of the architectural achievements of the early Islamic era.

Tracing the origins of civilization in Jordan reveals a mosaic of cultures and epochs. Each layer, each civilization, has contributed to the rich tapestry of Jordan's history. And this tapestry continues to be unraveled by the dedicated efforts of archaeologists, offering us ever-deepening insights into the remarkable civilizations that have called ancient Jordan their home.

The Nabateans: Guardians of Petra

In the heart of Jordan, concealed within the rose-red cliffs of southern Jordan, lies the ancient and enigmatic city of Petra. But to truly understand Petra's allure and the marvel that it represents, one must delve into the remarkable history of the people who crafted this stunning city out of rock – the Nabateans.

The Nabateans were an Arab nomadic tribe who settled in the region that we now know as southern Jordan around the 4th century BCE. It's a testament to their ingenuity and resourcefulness that they chose this seemingly inhospitable desert terrain as the canvas for their extraordinary masterpiece, Petra.

One of the defining characteristics of the Nabateans was their talent for water management. In a desert landscape where water was scarce and precious, they engineered a complex system of dams, channels, and cisterns to harness and distribute water throughout Petra. The ingenious engineering feats of the Nabateans allowed this once arid land to flourish, transforming it into a thriving oasis.

Petra itself is a testament to the Nabateans' architectural prowess. The city is famous for its intricate rock-cut facades, elaborate tombs, temples, and other structures that showcase their exceptional craftsmanship. The most iconic of these structures is the Treasury, or Al-Khazneh, with its breathtakingly detailed facade. This architectural marvel is a symbol of the wealth and power of the Nabatean civilization.

The Nabateans were also astute traders. Situated at the crossroads of important trade routes, Petra became a major trading hub for luxury goods such as spices, incense, silks, and precious metals. The city's prosperity was closely tied to its strategic location along these ancient trade networks.

What's equally remarkable is the Nabateans' adaptability and cosmopolitan outlook. Their culture absorbed influences from the various civilizations they interacted with, including the Greeks, Romans, and Egyptians. This cultural fusion is evident in the art, architecture, and inscriptions found throughout Petra.

While Petra thrived as the Nabatean capital, it also played a role in the broader geopolitical landscape. The Nabateans managed to maintain a degree of autonomy even as the Roman Empire expanded its influence in the region. It wasn't until 106 CE that Petra was finally annexed by Rome, marking the end of the Nabatean kingdom.

The decline of Petra as a major city came about with changes in trade routes and the shifting tides of history. Over time, the city was gradually abandoned and faded into obscurity, hidden beneath the sands of time.

Today, Petra stands as a testament to the enduring legacy of the Nabateans. It is a UNESCO World Heritage site and one of the most iconic archaeological wonders in the world. The indomitable spirit, innovative engineering, and artistic brilliance of the Nabateans continue to captivate and inspire those who venture into the breathtaking rose-red city they left behind.

Roman Influence in Jordan: From Jerash to Amman

In the annals of Jordan's history, the Roman era stands as a defining chapter that left an indelible mark on the landscape and culture of this ancient land. From the grandeur of Jerash to the transformation of Amman, Roman influence in Jordan was a pivotal force that shaped the region's destiny.

It was in the 1st century BCE that the Roman Republic, hungry for expansion and conquest, set its sights on the Eastern Mediterranean, including what is now Jordan. The strategic location of this region, at the crossroads of important trade routes and neighboring empires, made it a prize worth pursuing.

One of the most iconic Roman cities in Jordan is Jerash, known in antiquity as Gerasa. Founded by Alexander the Great's general Perdiccas, Jerash prospered under Roman rule. The city's stunning colonnaded streets, majestic temples, and grand theaters bear witness to the architectural splendor of the Roman era. The monumental Arch of Hadrian, built to honor the visit of the Roman Emperor Hadrian in 129 CE, still stands as a testament to the city's historical significance.

The Roman influence in Jordan extended beyond Jerash. The city of Philadelphia, modern-day Amman, also underwent a transformation during this period. Originally settled by the Ammonites and known as Rabbath-Ammon, it was renamed Philadelphia in honor of the Roman Emperor Philadelphus. The Roman administrators expanded and fortified the city, leaving behind an enduring legacy. One of the most prominent Roman remnants in Amman is the Amman Citadel, known as Jabal al-Qal'a. Perched on a hilltop, this historic site boasts a mix of Roman, Byzantine, and Umayyad structures. The Roman Temple of Hercules, with its colossal hand-shaped columns, is a testament to the city's Roman past.

But it wasn't just the architecture that bore the imprint of Rome. The Roman legal system, governance, and culture permeated Jordan during this period. The Pax Romana, a period of relative peace and stability, fostered economic growth and cultural exchange.

Jordan's strategic location along trade routes played a crucial role in connecting the Eastern Mediterranean to the Arabian Peninsula. Cities like Petra, although Nabatean in origin, also benefited from Roman influence as trade flourished and the region prospered.

The Roman era in Jordan was not without its challenges and upheavals. The Great Revolt of 66-70 CE and the subsequent destruction of Jerusalem had repercussions in the region, as did the gradual decline of the Roman Empire itself.

As the Roman Empire receded from its heights, the Byzantine Empire took its place, continuing to shape Jordan's cultural and religious landscape. The transition from Roman to Byzantine rule was marked by the spread of Christianity, leaving behind numerous churches and religious sites.

The Roman influence in Jordan remains an integral part of the country's historical tapestry. The archaeological treasures, architectural marvels, and the echoes of a bygone era serve as a testament to the enduring legacy of Roman rule. In the cities and landscapes of Jordan, the Roman imprint endures, inviting modern-day explorers to step back in time and discover the storied past of this remarkable land.

Islamic Heritage: Jordan's Role in Early Islamic History

In the early annals of Islamic history, Jordan occupies a significant and storied place. This land, which witnessed the rise and spread of Islam in its formative years, carries a rich heritage that is intertwined with the faith's growth and development.

The advent of Islam in the 7th century CE brought about a transformative period in the Arabian Peninsula and the surrounding regions. The Prophet Muhammad's message of monotheism and social justice resonated deeply with the people of the time, including those in present-day Jordan.

One of the pivotal moments in Islamic history occurred in the year 630 CE when the Prophet Muhammad led the Islamic community in the peaceful liberation of Mecca. This event marked a turning point for Islam, as the religion began to spread beyond the Arabian Peninsula.

Jordan, strategically located at the crossroads of major trade routes and with a diverse population, played a crucial role in the early Islamic expansion. The city of Tabuk, located in northern Jordan, was a significant stop on the Prophet Muhammad's journey during the Tabuk Expedition. This event is recorded in Islamic history as a test of faith and loyalty for the early Muslim community.

The region that is now Jordan was not only a transit point but also a place of settlement for early Muslim communities. Many tribes in the area embraced Islam, and over time, the faith became deeply ingrained in the culture and identity of the land.

Amman, the capital of Jordan today, traces its Islamic heritage back to this era. Originally known as Philadelphia, the city saw a transformation under early Islamic rule. The Umayyad Caliphate, based in Damascus, extended its influence to Amman and the surrounding region. The Umayyad Desert Castles, scattered across the desert landscapes of Jordan, bear witness to this period with their unique architectural features and intricate mosaics.

Jordan's geographical location also made it a vital crossroads for trade, culture, and intellectual exchange. The city of Kerak, for instance, played a role in the diffusion of knowledge during the Islamic Golden Age. Scholars and intellectuals from various corners of the Islamic world gathered here to exchange ideas and contribute to the flourishing of science, philosophy, and the arts.

The enduring legacy of early Islamic history in Jordan can be seen in the many historical sites, mosques, and cultural traditions that continue to thrive in the country. Mosques like the King Abdullah I Mosque in Amman stand as symbols of Islamic architecture and spiritual significance. The hospitality and warmth of the Jordanian people, often rooted in Islamic traditions of generosity and kindness, provide a living connection to this heritage.

Jordan's role in early Islamic history is a testament to the country's enduring connection to the faith and its contributions to the broader Islamic civilization. The echoes of the past resonate through the landscapes, culture, and people of Jordan, inviting visitors to explore the rich tapestry of its Islamic heritage.

The Crusades and Jordan: Echoes of Medieval Times

The Crusades were a series of religiously motivated military campaigns launched by Christian Europe in the 11th to 13th centuries. The aim was to recapture the Holy Land, including Jerusalem, from Muslim control. Jordan found itself at the heart of this epic clash of cultures and faiths.

One of the most iconic Crusader fortresses in Jordan is the imposing Karak Castle. Located in the town of Al-Karak, this medieval stronghold was built by the Crusaders in the 12th century atop the ruins of earlier fortifications, including those dating back to Roman and Byzantine times. Karak Castle was strategically positioned to control vital trade routes and served as a crucial military outpost for the Crusader kingdoms.

Kerak Castle became the epicenter of fierce battles and sieges during the Crusader period. Its walls witnessed the ebb and flow of power as it changed hands between Crusaders and Muslim forces multiple times. The castle's history is a testament to the relentless struggles that defined the Crusades in Jordan.

Other Crusader fortifications, such as Shobak Castle, also played a pivotal role in the region. These fortresses, perched on rugged hilltops, stood as both symbols of Christian military might and points of contention in the ongoing conflict.

Throughout the Crusader period, the landscape of Jordan was dotted with Christian settlements and churches. The Church of St. George in Madaba, with its intricate mosaic map of the Holy Land, offers a glimpse into the devotion of the Crusaders and their efforts to maintain a Christian presence in the region.

The Crusades in Jordan were not just about military conquest; they were also a time of cultural exchange. The intermingling of European, Arab, and Byzantine influences during this period left an indelible mark on the region's architecture, art, and traditions. Elements of Crusader architecture can still be seen in the design of some Jordanian buildings and castles.

It's important to note that the Crusader presence in Jordan was eventually curtailed, as Muslim forces, led by figures like Salah ad-Din (Saladin), regained control of the region. The legacy of the Crusades remains a complex and multifaceted part of Jordan's history, remembered through its fortresses, churches, and the stories passed down through generations.

Today, as you stand within the ancient stone walls of Karak Castle or explore the historical remnants of Crusader settlements, you can feel the echoes of medieval times. The Crusades in Jordan are a reminder of the enduring connections between East and West, faith and conflict, that have shaped this land throughout its storied history.

Ottoman Era: Jordan Under Ottoman Rule

In the grand tapestry of Jordan's history, the Ottoman era represents a pivotal and enduring chapter. It's a period that left an indelible mark on the land and its people, shaping the cultural, political, and architectural landscape in profound ways.

The Ottoman Empire, one of the most powerful and expansive empires in history, began its rule over Jordan in the early 16th century. This period of Ottoman dominance lasted for several centuries, up until the end of World War I when the empire dissolved.

One of the immediate effects of Ottoman rule was the reorganization of Jordan's administrative structure. The region was divided into provinces, or vilayets, with Amman serving as the capital of the southern part of the empire's Syria Vilayet. This administrative structure helped facilitate the empire's control over the region and its resources.

Under Ottoman rule, Jordan became an integral part of a vast network of trade routes. The famous Hejaz Railway, which connected Istanbul to the holy city of Medina, passed through Jordan, further solidifying the country's importance as a crossroads for commerce and travel. The Ottomans also left their architectural imprint on Jordan. The city of Salt, for example, boasts Ottoman-era houses adorned with distinctive architectural features such as arched windows and intricate wooden balconies. These houses reflect the architectural style of the period and serve as a living testament to the Ottoman influence. Amman, too, underwent transformation during the Ottoman era. The city was known as "Amman Fi al-Jabal," which translates to "Amman in the Mountains." Ottoman rulers undertook efforts to fortify and develop the city, and its strategic position along trade routes made it a vital center.

The Ottoman era also had profound implications for Jordan's demographics. The empire's policies led to the migration of various ethnic and religious groups into the region, further diversifying Jordan's population. Communities of Circassians, Chechens, and Bedouin tribes became part of the social fabric of the land.

Yet, Ottoman rule was not without its challenges and struggles. The empire faced political and economic difficulties in managing its vast territories, and this often translated into local unrest. In the late 19th and early 20th centuries, Jordan experienced a series of revolts and uprisings against Ottoman rule, reflecting the growing desire for self-determination.

The collapse of the Ottoman Empire at the end of World War I brought about a new chapter in Jordan's history, as the region came under British administration, eventually leading to the establishment of the Hashemite Kingdom of Jordan.

Today, Jordan's Ottoman legacy endures in its architecture, culture, and even in the names of many places and streets. The imprint of this era serves as a reminder of the enduring historical connections that have shaped the nation. The Ottoman era in Jordan, with its complexities and contradictions, stands as a testament to the country's rich and layered history.

The Birth of Modern Jordan: 20th Century History

The 20th century marked a transformative period in the history of Jordan, as the nation emerged from the ashes of the Ottoman Empire and navigated the complexities of the modern world. This era witnessed the birth of modern Jordan, a nation shaped by the forces of geopolitics, nationalism, and leadership.

Following the collapse of the Ottoman Empire at the end of World War I, Jordan came under British administration. It was part of the broader mandate system established by the League of Nations, with the British Mandate for Palestine including the territory of modern-day Jordan. During this period, the land that is now Jordan saw significant political, economic, and social changes.

One of the defining moments in Jordan's modern history was the Arab Revolt against Ottoman rule, led by figures like Sherif Hussein and his sons, including Abdullah. The Arab Revolt aimed to establish a unified Arab state and played a crucial role in the dismantling of Ottoman authority in the region. The aftermath of World War I saw the emergence of new borders and the division of territories. Transjordan, as it was known then, became a separate entity, distinct from Palestine, and Abdullah was appointed as its Emir. This marked the beginning of the Hashemite dynasty's rule in Jordan, a dynasty that continues to lead the nation today. The early decades of the 20th century were marked by efforts to establish stability and governance in Transjordan. Emir Abdullah, a visionary leader, laid the foundations for a modern state. His leadership saw the development of infrastructure, the establishment of educational institutions, and the creation of a sense of national identity. In 1946, Transjordan achieved full independence from Britain and was officially renamed the Hashemite Kingdom of Jordan. The newly independent nation faced numerous challenges, including the need to define its borders and establish diplomatic relations with neighboring countries.

One of the defining moments in Jordan's history came during the Arab-Israeli conflict of 1948-1949. Jordan played a significant role in the conflict, including the annexation of the West Bank. This move had far-reaching consequences for the nation's demographics and politics, as it absorbed Palestinian refugees. Over the ensuing decades, Jordan experienced periods of political and social transformation. The nation navigated the challenges of regional conflicts, including the Six-Day War of 1967 and the Yom Kippur War of 1973. Jordan also played a pivotal role in efforts to resolve the Israeli-Palestinian conflict, including its involvement in peace negotiations.

The latter part of the 20th century saw Jordan making strides in economic development and modernization. The nation's economy diversified, and there were investments in education, healthcare, and infrastructure.

Throughout these changes and challenges, the Hashemite monarchy remained a stabilizing force in Jordan, with successive kings leading the nation with a focus on modernization and reform.

The birth of modern Jordan in the 20th century is a testament to the resilience and adaptability of the nation and its people. It is a history marked by transitions, conflicts, and achievements, and it provides the backdrop for the Jordan we know today, a nation with a rich heritage and a promising future.

Contemporary Jordan: A Nation of Stability in the Middle East

In the tumultuous landscape of the Middle East, Jordan stands as a beacon of stability, a nation that has weathered regional challenges while forging its own unique path in the contemporary world. As we delve into the story of contemporary Jordan, we find a nation that has navigated the complexities of politics, economics, and society with resilience and pragmatism.

One of the defining features of contemporary Jordan is its status as a constitutional monarchy. The Hashemite monarchy, with King Abdullah II at its helm, has played a pivotal role in maintaining stability and unity within the country. The Hashemite lineage, dating back to Emir Abdullah's rule in the early 20th century, has provided a sense of continuity and legitimacy to the nation's leadership.

Jordan's foreign policy has been characterized by a commitment to peace and diplomacy in a region often marked by conflict. The nation played a pivotal role in the Arab Peace Initiative, advocating for a comprehensive resolution to the Israeli-Palestinian conflict. Additionally, Jordan has been a key ally of the United States and a partner in regional and international efforts to combat terrorism and promote stability.

The nation's commitment to diplomacy was further exemplified by its hosting of refugees from neighboring countries, particularly Palestinians and, more recently, Syrians. Jordan's refugee policy has been praised for its humanitarian approach, providing shelter and assistance to those fleeing conflict and persecution.

Economically, Jordan has undergone a process of liberalization and diversification. The nation has embraced economic reforms and sought to attract foreign investment. Efforts to develop sectors such as technology and renewable energy have been instrumental in the nation's economic growth.

Jordan's educational system has also seen significant development, with a focus on expanding access to quality education and vocational training. The country has invested in its human capital, fostering a skilled workforce that contributes to its economic development.

In recent years, Jordan has grappled with economic challenges, including high unemployment rates and fiscal deficits. However, the government has implemented reforms to address these issues, including subsidy reductions and efforts to improve the business environment.

The social fabric of contemporary Jordan reflects its diversity and cultural heritage. The nation is home to various ethnic and religious groups, including Jordanians of Palestinian, Bedouin, and Circassian descent, among others. This diversity is celebrated and protected by the constitution, which guarantees the rights of all citizens.

Jordan has also made strides in women's empowerment and gender equality, with efforts to increase women's participation in politics, education, and the workforce.

In the realm of culture, Jordan boasts a rich heritage that spans millennia. Its historical sites, such as Petra and Jerash, continue to attract tourists from around the world. The nation's commitment to preserving its cultural heritage is evident in its efforts to safeguard archaeological sites and promote cultural tourism.

Jordan's Natural Beauty: Landscapes and Wildlife

Jordan, a land steeped in history and culture, is also a place of remarkable natural beauty. Its diverse landscapes, from arid deserts to lush oases, offer a captivating tapestry of nature's wonders. As we explore Jordan's natural beauty, we discover a land that beckons adventurers and nature enthusiasts alike.

The heart of Jordan is the vast and mesmerizing desert landscape of Wadi Rum. Often referred to as the "Valley of the Moon," it is a place of stark, otherworldly beauty. Towering sandstone mountains and dunes, sculpted by the wind and time, create a surreal and ethereal atmosphere. Visitors can embark on jeep safaris, camel treks, or even hot air balloon rides to experience the grandeur of this desert wilderness.

Beyond the arid expanses, Jordan is blessed with a surprising contrast: the fertile Jordan Valley. Fed by the life-giving waters of the Jordan River, this lush region is a stark contrast to the surrounding desert. It is an agricultural paradise, where date palms, citrus orchards, and other crops thrive. The Jordan Valley is not only a source of sustenance but also a testament to the nation's ability to harness water resources for agriculture.

In the northwest, Jordan offers a refreshing respite in the form of the Ajloun Forest Reserve. This verdant sanctuary is a testament to Jordan's commitment to environmental conservation. Here, oak and pine forests provide habitat for diverse wildlife, including the rare and elusive Syrian wolf. Hiking trails meander through the reserve, offering glimpses of nature's beauty and tranquility.

For those seeking an underwater adventure, Jordan's coastline along the Red Sea is a treasure trove of marine life and coral reefs. The coastal town of Aqaba is a gateway to world-class scuba diving and snorkeling experiences. The vibrant coral gardens and diverse marine species, including colorful fish and sea turtles, make the Red Sea a haven for underwater enthusiasts.

The jewel in Jordan's natural crown is the Dead Sea, a unique saltwater lake that is the lowest point on Earth. Its hypersaline waters make floating effortless, and the mineral-rich mud is renowned for its therapeutic properties. The striking landscape of salt-crusted shores against the backdrop of barren hills creates an otherworldly ambiance.

Jordan's commitment to preserving its natural heritage is exemplified by its network of protected areas. Dana Biosphere Reserve, for instance, is a haven for biodiversity, home to a variety of wildlife, including ibex and eagles. This diverse ecosystem showcases the harmony between nature and human inhabitants who have lived here for centuries.

Jordanian Cuisine: A Delicious Blend of Flavors

Jordanian cuisine is a delightful tapestry of flavors, a culinary journey that reflects the nation's rich history, diverse culture, and the warmth of its people. As we explore the intricacies of Jordanian gastronomy, we uncover a delectable blend of traditional dishes and regional influences that have shaped this distinctive culinary heritage.

At the heart of Jordanian cuisine is a celebration of fresh and locally sourced ingredients. The cuisine embraces the flavors of the Mediterranean, Middle East, and North Africa, resulting in a harmonious fusion that pleases the palate.

One of the most iconic dishes of Jordan is Mansaf. This elaborate and savory dish consists of lamb cooked in a flavorful yogurt-based sauce, served over a bed of rice and garnished with toasted almonds and pine nuts. Mansaf is not just a meal; it's a symbol of hospitality and togetherness in Jordanian culture.

Another beloved dish is Maqluba, which translates to "upside-down" in Arabic. Maqluba is a layered dish of rice, vegetables, and meat (typically chicken or lamb), cooked in a pot, and then flipped upside-down when served. The result is a visually stunning and delicious medley of flavors and textures.

Falafel, crispy chickpea patties seasoned with aromatic herbs and spices, is a street food favorite in Jordan. Served in pita bread with fresh vegetables and tahini sauce, it's a satisfying and flavorful option for a quick meal.

Jordan's culinary repertoire also includes an array of delectable mezze, small dishes that are meant to be shared. Hummus, baba ghanoush, tabbouleh, and labneh are just a few of the mezze that grace Jordanian tables. These dishes showcase the art of simplicity and balance, with ingredients like olive oil, garlic, and herbs playing starring roles.

One cannot discuss Jordanian cuisine without mentioning the nation's love affair with olive oil. Jordan is blessed with fertile lands that yield some of the finest olive oil in the region. This golden elixir is not only a cooking staple but also a symbol of Jordan's connection to its land and heritage.

Jordan's sweet treats are equally enticing. Knafeh, a dessert made of shredded pastry soaked in syrup and layered with creamy cheese or clotted cream, is a beloved indulgence. The combination of crispy and sweet is a sensory delight.

Mint tea, served in tiny glass cups, is the beverage of choice for many Jordanians. The refreshing and aromatic tea is often accompanied by dates or other sweets, making it a cherished part of daily life.

Beyond its traditional dishes, Jordanian cuisine has embraced culinary innovation and international influences. Visitors to Jordan can explore a thriving food scene that includes international restaurants, modern cafes, and street food stalls that offer a taste of the world's flavors.

Jordanian cuisine is not just about food; it's a cultural expression, a reflection of the nation's history and values. The act of sharing a meal in Jordan is a cherished tradition that fosters connections and embodies the warmth of the people. It's an invitation to savor the delicious blend of flavors that make Jordanian cuisine a truly exceptional culinary experience.

A Culinary Journey: Traditional Jordanian Dishes

Embarking on a culinary journey through Jordan means immersing yourself in a world of traditional dishes that have been perfected over centuries. These time-honored recipes are more than just food; they are a celebration of Jordan's culture, history, and the heartwarming hospitality of its people.

Mansaf: At the pinnacle of Jordanian cuisine sits Mansaf, a dish of profound significance. This savory masterpiece features tender lamb, slow-cooked to perfection, and adorned with a luxurious sauce made from yogurt and dried, fermented yogurt balls called "jameed." The dish is typically served over a bed of fragrant rice, garnished with almonds and pine nuts. Mansaf is often enjoyed on special occasions, symbolizing the spirit of togetherness and generosity that defines Jordanian hospitality.

Maqluba: Maqluba, which translates to "upside-down" in Arabic, is both a culinary delight and a visual spectacle. This dish showcases layers of rice, vegetables, and meat, usually chicken or lamb, cooked together in a single pot. When it's time to serve, the pot is flipped upside-down onto a large platter, creating a stunning mosaic of colors and flavors. Maqluba embodies the essence of family gatherings and communal feasting.

Kebabs and Grilled Meats: The sizzle of kebabs on an open grill is a familiar and irresistible sound in Jordan. These skewered delights come in various forms, from succulent lamb skewers seasoned with aromatic spices to minced meat kebabs known as "kafta." Grilled meats are often accompanied by warm pita bread, fresh vegetables, and a drizzle of tahini or yogurt sauce.

Falafel: Falafel, those golden-brown orbs of chickpea or fava bean goodness, are a staple of Jordanian street food. These crispy, flavorful patties are created from ground legumes blended with an array of herbs and spices. Served in pita bread with a colorful array of fresh vegetables and creamy tahini sauce, falafel is a quick and satisfying meal that captures the essence of Jordan's culinary scene.

Mezze: Jordan's culinary tradition shines brightly in its mezze, a collection of small, flavorful dishes meant to be shared among friends and family. Hummus, a creamy blend of chickpeas, tahini, and lemon juice, is a beloved classic. Baba ghanoush, made from roasted eggplants, showcases a smoky depth of flavor. Tabbouleh, a vibrant salad of parsley, bulgur, tomatoes, and herbs, adds a refreshing element to the mezze spread. These dishes celebrate the art of simplicity and balance, embodying the essence of Jordanian cuisine.

Olive Oil: Olive oil is more than just a cooking ingredient in Jordan; it's a cultural treasure. The country's fertile lands yield some of the finest olive oil in the region. This golden elixir is used generously in Jordanian cooking, imparting a rich, fruity flavor to dishes and salads. The olive tree is a symbol of abundance and peace, and the olive branch adorns the nation's flag.

Sweet Delights: A Jordanian meal is never complete without a touch of sweetness. Knafeh, a dessert made from shredded pastry soaked in syrup and layered with creamy cheese or clotted cream, is a cherished indulgence. It's a dessert that embodies the perfect balance of crispy and sweet, leaving a lasting impression on the taste buds.

As you embark on your culinary journey through Jordan, these traditional dishes will be your guideposts. They are the embodiment of a culture that celebrates family, hospitality, and the art of savoring life's flavors. Jordanian cuisine invites you to take a seat at the table, share a meal, and savor the timeless tastes of this captivating land.

Must-Try Jordanian Desserts and Beverages

Exploring the sweet side of Jordanian cuisine is a journey into a world of delightful flavors and time-honored traditions. The nation's desserts and beverages are a testament to its rich culinary heritage, where every bite and sip tells a story of craftsmanship and culture.

Knafeh: Knafeh, often hailed as the queen of Jordanian desserts, is a symphony of textures and tastes. This beloved dessert is made from layers of shredded pastry soaked in fragrant syrup, with a luscious filling of creamy cheese or clotted cream. The result is a delightful contrast between the crispy, golden exterior and the sweet, gooey interior. Knafeh is often garnished with crushed pistachios for added flavor and a touch of color.

Basbousa: Basbousa is a simple yet satisfying dessert that finds its way into many Jordanian homes and gatherings. It consists of a semolina cake soaked in rose or orange blossom water syrup, which gives it a fragrant and slightly floral aroma. The cake is often garnished with blanched almonds or coconut flakes, adding a delightful crunch to each bite.

Atayef: Atayef are small, folded pancakes that are traditionally enjoyed during the holy month of Ramadan. These mini pancakes are filled with various sweet fillings, such as sweet cheese, ashta (clotted cream), or a mixture of nuts and sugar. Once folded, they are often drizzled with orange blossom or rose water syrup, infusing them with a delightful floral essence.

Qatayef: Similar in name but distinct in preparation from Atayef, Qatayef is a dessert made from thin, crepe-like pancakes filled with various sweet fillings. The fillings can range from nuts and honey to cheese or cream. Qatayef can be served folded or open, and they are a favorite during special occasions and festive gatherings.

Arabic Coffee: Arabic coffee, known as "gahwa" or "qahwa," is an integral part of Jordanian hospitality. This strong and aromatic coffee is traditionally brewed with lightly roasted coffee beans and infused with cardamom. It is typically served in small, handleless cups along with dates, symbolizing a warm welcome to guests.

Mint Tea: Mint tea, or "shai na'na," is a refreshing beverage that is widely enjoyed in Jordan. Fresh mint leaves are steeped in boiling water and sweetened with sugar to create a fragrant and revitalizing drink. It is often served in small glass cups, and its soothing qualities make it a perfect choice after a hearty meal.

Tamarind Juice: Tamarind juice, known as "tamr hindi," is a tangy and refreshing beverage made from the pulp of the tamarind fruit. The tartness of tamarind is balanced with sugar and water to create a cooling and revitalizing drink, especially popular during hot Jordanian summers.

Exploring Jordanian desserts and beverages is not just a culinary adventure; it's an immersion into the heart and soul of the country's culture. These sweet creations and aromatic brews are a testament to the importance of hospitality and the joy of savoring life's simple pleasures. Whether it's the decadence of Knafeh, the floral notes of Basbousa, or the comforting sips of mint tea, Jordanian desserts and beverages offer a taste of tradition and a glimpse into the warmth of Jordanian hospitality.

Jordan's Vineyards: Wine and Viticulture

Nestled in the heart of the Middle East, Jordan may not be the first place that comes to mind when you think of wine production, but this ancient land has a rich history of viticulture that dates back thousands of years. Jordan's vineyards are a testament to its ability to produce wine of exceptional quality and flavor.

Historical Roots: Wine has a deep-rooted history in Jordan, dating back to ancient times. Archaeological evidence reveals that wine was produced here as far back as 4000 BC. The region's favorable climate and fertile soil made it an ideal place for cultivating grapes and crafting wine.

Modern Revival: While Jordan's wine industry faced challenges in the 20th century, it has experienced a resurgence in recent decades. Today, the country boasts modern vineyards and wineries that produce a variety of wines, including both red and white varietals.

Wine Varietals: Jordan's vineyards are known for cultivating several grape varietals, each contributing its unique character to the wines. Cabernet Sauvignon, Merlot, and Syrah are popular choices for red wines, known for their bold flavors and aromas. For white wines, Chardonnay and Sauvignon Blanc are commonly grown, offering a refreshing and crisp taste.

Distinct Terroir: The concept of terroir, which encompasses the environmental factors that influence wine flavor, is evident in Jordan's wines. The country's vineyards benefit from a diverse landscape that includes mountains, valleys, and the Jordan River. These geographical features, combined with the Mediterranean climate, impart a distinct character to Jordanian wines.

Winemaking Craftsmanship: Jordan's winemakers have honed their craft to produce wines of exceptional quality. Modern winemaking techniques, combined with respect for tradition, result in wines that are both elegant and expressive. Some wineries even incorporate ancient methods, such as clay amphorae for fermentation, as a nod to the country's historical winemaking heritage.

Awards and Recognition: Jordanian wines have gained recognition on the international stage. They have received awards and accolades, which serve as a testament to the country's winemaking prowess. Jordanian wineries continue to strive for excellence, aiming to further establish their presence in the global wine market.

Wine Tourism: Jordan's vineyards have become a popular destination for wine enthusiasts and tourists. Visitors can tour the wineries, witness the winemaking process, and, of course, indulge in tastings of the finest Jordanian wines. The picturesque landscapes of vine-covered hills add to the allure of wine tourism in Jordan.

Cultural Significance: Wine holds cultural significance in Jordan, often being an integral part of celebrations and gatherings. It symbolizes hospitality, togetherness, and a connection to the land. Sharing a bottle of Jordanian wine is a way of forging bonds and creating lasting memories.

Jordan's vineyards, with their deep historical roots and modern innovations, have carved a unique niche in the world of wine production. They embody the spirit of a country that cherishes its past while embracing the future. The wines that emerge from these vineyards are not just beverages; they are a reflection of Jordan's terroir, craftsmanship, and the enduring legacy of viticulture in this remarkable land.

Petra: The Rose-Red City of Ancient Wonders

Hidden away in the rugged deserts of Jordan lies an archaeological marvel that has captured the imaginations of travelers, historians, and adventurers for centuries. Petra, often referred to as the "Rose-Red City," stands as a testament to the ingenuity and craftsmanship of an ancient civilization that carved a city into the rose-hued cliffs of southern Jordan.

A Lost City Rediscovered: For centuries, Petra remained shrouded in mystery, known primarily to local Bedouin communities. It wasn't until the early 19th century that Swiss explorer Johann Ludwig Burckhardt stumbled upon this hidden treasure. His rediscovery of Petra captivated the world and sparked an era of exploration and fascination.

Ancient Origins: Petra's history is deeply rooted in antiquity. It was the capital of the Nabatean Kingdom, a powerful and enigmatic civilization that thrived from the 4th century BC to the 2nd century AD. The Nabateans were skilled traders who controlled vital caravan routes, amassing wealth and influence.

The Rose-Red Hue: One of the most striking features of Petra is the rosy hue of its rock-cut architecture. The city's structures were carved directly into the naturally occurring rose-red sandstone cliffs, giving rise to its nickname, the "Rose-Red City." The colors of the rock formations change with the shifting sunlight, creating a mesmerizing play of shades and shadows.

The Treasury (Al-Khazneh): Arguably the most famous building in Petra is the Treasury, known as Al-Khazneh in Arabic. This iconic façade, carved into the cliff face, served as a tomb and ceremonial structure. Its intricate design, featuring columns, statues, and intricate reliefs, is a testament to the architectural prowess of the Nabateans. The Treasury's name comes from the legend that it once held hidden treasures, though no such riches have ever been found.

The Siq: To reach the Treasury, visitors must traverse a narrow, winding gorge known as the Siq. This natural corridor, flanked by towering cliffs, creates a dramatic and awe-inspiring approach to Petra's main attraction. As you journey through the Siq, the anticipation builds, leading to the grand reveal of the Treasury at its end.

The Monastery (Ad-Deir): Beyond the Treasury, Petra unfolds further treasures. The Monastery, or Ad-Deir, is another remarkable structure carved into the cliffs. Its grand façade, reached by climbing a series of steps, showcases a similar level of craftsmanship as the Treasury. The Monastery is a testament to the skill and dedication of the Nabatean builders.

Ancient Engineering Marvels: Petra is not just about its stunning façades; it's also a showcase of ancient engineering marvels. The city's sophisticated water management system, which included dams, cisterns, and aqueducts, enabled its inhabitants to thrive in a region with limited water resources.

UNESCO World Heritage Site: In 1985, Petra was designated a UNESCO World Heritage Site, recognizing its historical and cultural significance. It has since become one of the most visited archaeological sites in the world, drawing travelers from all corners of the globe.

Petra's allure lies not only in its remarkable architecture but also in the air of mystery that surrounds it. Despite centuries of exploration, the city continues to reveal its secrets, making it a destination that beckons adventurers and history enthusiasts alike. Petra is a testament to the enduring legacy of the Nabateans and the awe-inspiring beauty of ancient wonders carved into the very heart of the desert.

The Dead Sea: Earth's Lowest Point and Natural Wonder

Nestled between the borders of Jordan and Israel lies a natural wonder of unparalleled uniqueness—the Dead Sea. This extraordinary body of water, often dubbed Earth's lowest point, is a geological marvel that has fascinated humanity for centuries.

The Lowest Point on Earth: The Dead Sea holds the impressive distinction of being the lowest point on the Earth's surface, situated approximately 1,410 feet (430 meters) below sea level. This natural depression forms part of the larger Jordan Rift Valley, a geological feature shaped by the movement of tectonic plates.

A Saltwater Lake: Despite its name, the Dead Sea is not a sea but rather a saltwater lake. Its extremely high salt content—around 34.2% salinity—makes it nearly 10 times saltier than ordinary seawater. This salinity is a result of the lake's unique geological history and its lack of an outlet, which causes minerals and salts to accumulate over time.

Unsinkable Floating Experience: One of the Dead Sea's most famous features is its remarkable buoyancy. Thanks to its high salinity, swimmers effortlessly float on the surface, experiencing a sensation of weightlessness. It's a truly unique and almost surreal experience that draws visitors from around the world. **Therapeutic Properties**: The minerals and salts found in the Dead Sea mud and water have long been believed to have therapeutic properties. People have traveled to its shores for millennia to take advantage of its purported health benefits. The mineral-rich mud is often used for natural skincare treatments and is thought to help with skin conditions like psoriasis and eczema. **A Unique Ecosystem**: Despite its extreme salinity, the Dead Sea is not entirely lifeless. Certain types of microorganisms and algae have adapted to thrive in its harsh conditions. These microorganisms are responsible for the lake's striking red and orange hues in some areas.

Shrinking Water Levels: Over the years, the Dead Sea has been shrinking at an alarming rate due to a combination of factors, including the diversion of its main water source, the Jordan River, for agriculture and industrial use. The declining water levels have caused environmental concerns and prompted conservation efforts to stabilize the lake's ecosystem.

Mineral Extraction: The Dead Sea is a rich source of minerals, including magnesium, calcium, and potassium. These minerals are extracted from the lake for use in various industries, including cosmetics and fertilizers. The economic importance of these resources adds to the complexity of managing the lake's delicate ecosystem.

A Geological Time Capsule: The mud and rock formations around the Dead Sea preserve a remarkable geological record, with layers dating back thousands of years. Scientists study these layers to gain insights into the Earth's history and the changes that have occurred in this region over millennia.

The Dead Sea stands as a testament to the marvels of our planet's natural wonders. Its extreme salinity, therapeutic properties, and unique ecosystem have captured the imagination of explorers and scientists alike. As a place of both geological significance and natural beauty, the Dead Sea continues to be a source of fascination and wonder for those who venture to its shores.

Wadi Rum: The Desert of Lawrence of Arabia

Nestled in the southern reaches of Jordan, Wadi Rum stands as a desert landscape of legendary proportions. This vast and mesmerizing expanse of sandstone and granite has captured the hearts of adventurers, filmmakers, and dreamers alike. It's a place where the timeless beauty of the desert meets the echoes of history, most notably through the connection with the enigmatic figure of Lawrence of Arabia.

A Geological Masterpiece: Wadi Rum's geological tapestry is nothing short of awe-inspiring. It's a desert sculpted by nature's hand, with towering sandstone mountains, narrow canyons, and vast, open valleys. The wind and erosion have shaped these rock formations into a surreal and otherworldly landscape that feels like something out of a science fiction novel.

The Land of Lawrence: Wadi Rum's association with T.E. Lawrence, the British archaeologist, army officer, and diplomat who became a legendary figure during World War I, is a key part of its allure. Lawrence of Arabia's time spent in Wadi Rum is immortalized in his autobiographical writings and later in the epic film "Lawrence of Arabia." Visitors to Wadi Rum can explore the very desert where Lawrence once rode with Bedouin allies.

Bedouin Heritage: Wadi Rum is home to the Zalabia Bedouin, a nomadic people who have inhabited this desert for generations. Their knowledge of the desert's secrets and their unique way of life are an integral part of the Wadi Rum experience. Visitors can immerse themselves in Bedouin hospitality, learn about their traditions, and even embark on desert journeys guided by Bedouin hosts. **Starry Skies**: Wadi Rum's remote location and minimal light pollution make it one of the world's premier stargazing destinations. The desert's clear, dark skies provide an unparalleled canvas for observing the cosmos. It's a place where you can gaze up at the Milky Way and see stars in such abundance that they seem to outnumber the grains of sand below.

Desert Adventures: Wadi Rum offers a playground for outdoor enthusiasts. Activities such as rock climbing, hiking, and jeep tours allow visitors to explore its natural wonders up close. Scaling the sandstone cliffs or traversing the desert in a 4x4 vehicle provide a sense of adventure that's hard to replicate elsewhere.

Filmmaker's Paradise: The striking and otherworldly landscapes of Wadi Rum have served as the backdrop for numerous films, including not only "Lawrence of Arabia" but also more recent blockbusters like "The Martian." Filmmakers are drawn to the desert's cinematic qualities, and it's not difficult to see why.

A Timeless Oasis: Wadi Rum's beauty is timeless. The shifting sands, the play of light on the rocks, and the vastness of the desert create an ever-changing panorama that enchants those who venture here. It's a place where you can escape the hustle and bustle of modern life and connect with the ancient rhythms of the desert.

Wadi Rum is more than a desert; it's a dreamscape where reality blends with the surreal. It's a testament to the enduring allure of the Arabian wilderness and the echoes of history that linger in its sands. Lawrence of Arabia found inspiration here, and so do countless others who seek the magic of this desert of legend.

Exploring the Dana Biosphere Reserve

Nestled in the rugged heart of Jordan, the Dana Biosphere Reserve unfolds as a breathtaking testament to the country's natural beauty and ecological diversity. Stretching from the heights of the Jordan Rift Valley to the desert lowlands, Dana is the largest biosphere reserve in Jordan and a place of both ecological significance and natural wonder.

Diverse Ecosystems: The Dana Biosphere Reserve boasts a remarkable range of ecosystems, from the snow-capped peaks of the Shara Mountains to the arid desert expanses below. This diversity of habitats is a haven for a wide array of plant and animal species, many of which are adapted to the harsh desert environment.

Wildlife Sanctuary: Dana is home to numerous rare and endangered species, making it a critical wildlife sanctuary in the region. Visitors may spot iconic desert wildlife such as the Nubian ibex, Syrian wolf, and sand fox. Birdwatchers are also in for a treat, as the reserve is a migratory corridor for various bird species.

Hiking Haven: For adventure seekers and nature enthusiasts, Dana offers an extensive network of hiking trails that wind through its dramatic landscapes. The Dana to Petra trek, a multi-day journey, is a favorite among hikers. It takes you through rugged canyons, past ancient ruins, and offers panoramic views of the reserve's diverse terrain. **Cultural Heritage**: Dana is not just a place of natural beauty; it also holds a rich cultural heritage. The region has been inhabited for thousands of years, and evidence of ancient civilizations, including Nabatean and Roman ruins, can be found within the reserve. The local Bedouin communities add to the cultural tapestry, and visitors can learn about their traditional way of life.

Conservation Efforts: Conservation is at the heart of Dana's mission. Efforts to protect the fragile ecosystems and wildlife are ongoing. The reserve serves as a model for sustainable development, balancing the needs of the environment with those of the local communities.

Stargazer's Paradise: With its remote location and minimal light pollution, Dana is a prime spot for stargazing. On clear nights, the sky lights up with a dazzling display of stars and constellations, offering an unforgettable celestial experience.

A Desert Oasis: Despite the arid surroundings, Dana is not devoid of water. Natural springs and streams provide a lifeline for the flora and fauna of the region. These water sources create pockets of lush vegetation and serve as crucial watering holes.

Visitor's Center: The Dana Biosphere Reserve has a visitor's center that serves as an educational hub. Here, you can learn about the reserve's ecosystems, wildlife, and the ongoing conservation efforts. Knowledgeable staff are on hand to answer questions and provide guidance to visitors.

Exploring the Dana Biosphere Reserve is a journey into the heart of Jordan's natural beauty and ecological significance. It's a place where the stark beauty of the desert meets the vibrancy of life, where ancient traditions and modern conservation efforts coexist, and where the wonders of the natural world unfold in all their glory. Dana invites you to immerse yourself in its diverse landscapes and discover the hidden treasures of this extraordinary biosphere reserve.

Aqaba: Jordan's Gateway to the Red Sea

Nestled along Jordan's southernmost coastline lies Aqaba, a city of strategic importance and natural beauty that serves as the nation's gateway to the Red Sea. This bustling port city, with its rich history and vibrant marine life, offers a unique blend of culture, commerce, and coastal allure.

Historical Significance: Aqaba's history dates back thousands of years, making it one of the world's oldest continuously inhabited cities. It has witnessed the passage of civilizations, from the ancient Egyptians and Nabateans to the Romans and Ottomans. The city's strategic location at the crossroads of trade routes has contributed to its enduring importance.

Port of Vital Importance: As Jordan's only coastal city, Aqaba holds immense economic and strategic value. Its port, the Aqaba Port, is a lifeline for the country's trade, connecting Jordan to international markets. The port handles various cargo, including goods bound for Jordan and neighboring countries.

Red Sea Beauty: Aqaba's coastline along the Red Sea is a magnet for divers and snorkelers. The Red Sea's crystal-clear waters are teeming with vibrant coral reefs and a kaleidoscope of marine life. Divers have the opportunity to explore some of the world's most renowned dive sites, including the Japanese Garden and the Cedar Pride wreck.

Underwater Treasures: The Red Sea is renowned for its diverse marine ecosystem. Divers and snorkelers can encounter a stunning array of marine species, including colorful fish, turtles, and even the occasional dolphins. The vibrant coral gardens are a testament to the Red Sea's status as a global marine biodiversity hotspot.

Water Sports Paradise: Beyond diving, Aqaba offers a wide range of water sports activities. Windsurfing, kiteboarding, and jet-skiing enthusiasts flock to the city's shores to ride the Red Sea's winds and waves. The warm waters and consistent winds make Aqaba an ideal playground for water sports.

Historical Sites: Aqaba's historic sites bear witness to its rich past. The Aqaba Fort, also known as the Mamluk Castle, is a prominent landmark. Dating back to the 16th century, it was once part of the city's defenses and today serves as a museum that offers insights into Aqaba's history.

Cultural Melting Pot: Aqaba's diverse population includes Jordanians, Bedouins, and expatriates, creating a vibrant cultural tapestry. Visitors can savor a wide range of cuisines, from traditional Jordanian dishes to international fare, at the city's restaurants and cafes.

Gateway to Jordan's Treasures: Aqaba's location makes it an ideal starting point for exploring Jordan's many wonders. From here, travelers can embark on journeys to Petra, the Dead Sea, Wadi Rum, and other iconic destinations. Aqaba serves as the entryway to the country's diverse landscapes and cultural heritage.

Aqaba's blend of history, commerce, and natural beauty makes it a unique destination on Jordan's map. Whether you're drawn to its ancient sites, the allure of the Red Sea, or the warm hospitality of its people, Aqaba invites you to explore its many facets and experience the harmony of tradition and modernity along Jordan's coastal gem.

Amman: The Capital City's Rich Heritage

At the heart of Jordan, amid rolling hills and ancient landscapes, lies Amman, the vibrant capital city that weaves together the threads of history and modernity in a rich tapestry of culture and heritage.

A City of Ancient Origins: Amman's roots stretch far back in time. Originally known as Philadelphia, the city was founded by the Ptolemies in the 3rd century BC. Its strategic location along trade routes made it a coveted prize for various empires, including the Romans, Byzantines, and Umayyads.

Roman Ruins: Evidence of Amman's Roman past can still be seen today. The Amman Citadel, perched atop Jabal al-Qal'a, showcases well-preserved Roman ruins, including the Temple of Hercules and the Umayyad Palace. These remnants of the past offer a glimpse into the city's ancient glory.

Modern Metropolis: Amman has evolved into a thriving modern metropolis while preserving its historical heritage. The city's skyline is a blend of modern high-rises and traditional architecture, where glass skyscrapers stand alongside markets and souks that have existed for centuries.

Cultural Melting Pot: Amman's diverse population reflects the cultural tapestry of Jordan. People from various backgrounds and walks of life call the city home. This diversity is reflected in the cuisine, languages spoken, and the arts and culture that flourish in its streets.

Historic Downtown: Downtown Amman, often referred to as Al-Balad, is a bustling hub of activity. Here, you can explore the vibrant markets of Souk Al-Bukharia and sample traditional Jordanian dishes at local eateries. The historical Raghadan Flagpole and the Roman Theater add to the area's charm.

Museums and Galleries: Amman boasts a rich cultural scene with numerous museums and art galleries. The Jordan Museum offers a deep dive into the country's history and archaeology. The Royal Automobile Museum showcases a collection of vintage cars, including those owned by the royal family.

A Modern Capital: Amman is not just about its historical treasures; it's a city that embraces modernity. The upscale district of Abdoun offers luxury shopping and fine dining. The city's nightlife scene is lively, with a range of bars, clubs, and entertainment venues.

The People's Warmth: One of Amman's most endearing qualities is the warmth of its people. Jordanians are known for their hospitality and friendliness. Visitors often find themselves welcomed with open arms and offered a cup of traditional Arabic coffee or tea.

Gateway to Jordan: Amman serves as a gateway to Jordan's many attractions. It's the starting point for exploring Petra, the Dead Sea, Wadi Rum, and other iconic destinations. The city's central location makes it an ideal base for travelers eager to experience the country's diverse landscapes.

Amman is a city where the past gracefully mingles with the present, where modernity and tradition coexist in harmony. It's a place where you can wander through ancient ruins in the morning and dine at a trendy restaurant in the evening. In Amman, the stories of history, the vibrancy of culture, and the warmth of its people come together to create a truly unique and captivating capital city.

Historic City of Jerash: A Window to the Past

Nestled in the northern part of Jordan, the historic city of Jerash stands as a mesmerizing window to the past, offering visitors a captivating glimpse into the grandeur of antiquity. With its well-preserved ruins, grand colonnades, and an aura that seems frozen in time, Jerash is an archaeological treasure trove that transports you back to the days of the Roman Empire.

A Rich History Unearthed: Jerash's history dates back millennia, with evidence of human habitation from as early as the Bronze Age. However, it was during the Greco-Roman period that the city truly flourished. Known in antiquity as Gerasa, it was a prominent member of the Decapolis, a league of ten cities in the eastern Roman Empire.

Roman Splendor: The most striking aspect of Jerash is its remarkably well-preserved Roman architecture. The city's Oval Plaza, flanked by majestic colonnades, serves as the heart of the archaeological site. Walking along the cobbled streets, you can imagine the bustling markets, vibrant processions, and cultural exchanges that once took place here.

The Triumphal Arch: The Arch of Hadrian, built to honor the visit of Emperor Hadrian in the 2nd century AD, is a splendid testament to Roman engineering and craftsmanship. Its intricate detailing and towering presence make it one of Jerash's most iconic landmarks.

The South Theater: Jerash boasts two remarkably preserved Roman theaters, with the South Theater being the larger of the two. With its tiered seating and capacity to hold thousands, it once hosted grand performances and gatherings. Today, it continues to serve as a venue for cultural events and concerts.

Cardo Maximus: The main north-south street, known as the Cardo Maximus, is flanked by Ionic columns and lined with shops and storefronts. It's a vivid reminder of the city's commercial vibrancy during its heyday.

Hadrian's Temple: The Temple of Artemis and the Temple of Zeus, along with the Nymphaeum and the Temple of Hadrian, are further testaments to the religious and architectural prowess of the time. Their intricate carvings and grandeur transport visitors to an era of devotion and artistic excellence.

A Journey Through Time: Jerash's archaeological significance extends beyond the Roman period, with remnants from Byzantine and early Islamic eras. It offers a layered history where different civilizations left their mark on the city's landscape.

A Living Archaeology: What makes Jerash even more remarkable is that it's not just a relic of the past; it's a living archaeological site. Visitors can experience its history through cultural festivals, reenactments, and performances that bring the ancient city to life.

A UNESCO World Heritage Site: In recognition of its historical significance and exceptional preservation, Jerash was designated a UNESCO World Heritage Site in 1982. It stands as a testament to the importance of safeguarding and celebrating our shared human heritage.

Jerash is more than a city frozen in time; it's a testament to the enduring legacy of human civilization. As you stroll through its ancient streets, you can't help but be transported back in time, imagining the lives and stories of the people who once called this remarkable place home. Jerash is a treasure trove of history, an open book waiting to be explored, and a vivid reminder of the grandeur of the past.

Madaba: City of Mosaics

Nestled in the heart of Jordan, the city of Madaba is a captivating mosaic of history, culture, and artistry. Known as the "City of Mosaics," Madaba is a treasure trove of ancient craftsmanship, where every stone tells a story and every mosaic is a masterpiece.

A Tapestry of Antiquity: Madaba's history stretches back thousands of years, with archaeological evidence suggesting habitation as far back as the Bronze Age. However, it's the city's remarkable mosaic heritage that has earned it worldwide recognition.

The Famous Madaba Map: The crowning jewel of Madaba is undoubtedly the Madaba Map, an ancient mosaic map of the Holy Land that dates back to the 6th century AD. Housed in the Greek Orthodox Church of St. George, this mosaic is a marvel of craftsmanship and a priceless historical document. It offers a detailed representation of Jerusalem, providing valuable insights into the geography and religious significance of the region.

Mosaics Everywhere: While the Madaba Map is the most famous, it's just the tip of the iceberg. Madaba is adorned with numerous mosaics that grace its churches, homes, and public spaces. These intricate artworks depict scenes from biblical stories, historical events, and daily life in antiquity.

Churches and Shrines: Madaba is home to a rich collection of churches and shrines, each housing exquisite mosaics. The Church of the Apostles, the Church of the Virgin Mary, and the Church of the Beheading of St. John the Baptist are just a few examples. These places of worship offer visitors a chance to marvel at the artistry of ancient craftsmen.

A Cultural Crossroads: Madaba's mosaic tradition reflects its position as a crossroads of civilizations. Over the centuries, it has been influenced by Roman, Byzantine, Islamic, and Crusader cultures. This cultural fusion is evident in the variety of mosaic designs and themes.

Modern Mosaic Craftsmanship: While Madaba is steeped in history, it's also a hub of contemporary mosaic artistry. Skilled craftsmen in the city continue to create intricate mosaics, blending tradition with innovation. Visitors can witness the mosaic-making process in workshops and even try their hand at this ancient art form.

The Madaba Experience: Exploring Madaba is like stepping into a living museum of mosaics. As you wander through its streets, you'll come across mosaics embedded in sidewalks, walls, and courtyards. The city's mosaic heritage is not confined to museums but is an integral part of daily life.

A Mosaic Legacy: Madaba's commitment to preserving its mosaic heritage is evident through ongoing restoration efforts and the establishment of the Madaba Mosaic School. This school trains a new generation of mosaic artists, ensuring that this ancient craft continues to flourish.

Madaba, the "City of Mosaics," is a living testament to the enduring artistry of mosaic craftsmen throughout the ages. It's a place where history comes to life through intricate designs, where every mosaic tells a tale of a bygone era. Madaba invites you to explore its streets, churches, and workshops, where the vibrant tradition of mosaic art continues to thrive, preserving the city's rich cultural heritage for generations to come.

Karak Castle: A Fortress of Endurance

High atop a hill in the heart of Jordan, Karak Castle stands as a symbol of endurance, a sentinel of history, and a testament to the resilience of those who built and defended it. This imposing fortress, also known as Al-Karak Castle, has weathered centuries of challenges, battles, and conquests, earning its place as one of the most remarkable historical sites in the region.

Ancient Origins: Karak Castle's origins trace back to the time of the Crusaders, who constructed this formidable fortress in the 12th century. Strategically perched on a hill, it served as a crucial stronghold for both Crusaders and later Islamic rulers.

Crusader Stronghold: During the Crusades, Karak Castle played a pivotal role in the region's tumultuous history. It changed hands multiple times, with Crusaders, Ayyubids, and Mamluks vying for control. The castle's design, featuring thick walls, towers, and a maze-like layout, made it a formidable defensive structure.

Ayyubid and Mamluk Rule: Under the Ayyubid and Mamluk dynasties, Karak Castle saw periods of expansion and renovation. The Ayyubid ruler Salah ad-Din (Saladin) himself captured the fortress in 1188, marking a significant moment in its history.

A Blend of Architectural Styles: Karak Castle showcases a unique blend of architectural styles, reflecting the diverse cultures and rulers who left their mark on it. Its massive walls, arrow slits, and deep cisterns are a testament to the castle's military significance.

The Underground Passageways: One of the most intriguing features of Karak Castle is its network of underground passageways and tunnels. These tunnels served various purposes, from providing access to water sources to enabling stealthy movement during sieges.

The Iconic Crusader Church: Within the castle's walls, visitors can explore the remains of a Crusader church. Its architectural details and the atmospheric setting make it a site of historical and archaeological significance.

An Ongoing Legacy: Today, Karak Castle stands as a heritage site and a vivid reminder of Jordan's rich history. Its well-preserved structure allows visitors to step back in time and imagine the events that unfolded within its walls.

A UNESCO World Heritage Nominee: Karak Castle has been recognized for its historical and architectural importance, earning a nomination for UNESCO World Heritage status. Its inclusion on this prestigious list would further highlight its significance on the world stage.

A Visitor's Journey: Exploring Karak Castle is a journey through time, where you can walk along ancient walls, descend into dark tunnels, and soak in panoramic views of the surrounding landscape. It's a place where history comes to life, and where the stories of knights, rulers, and conquerors echo through the ages.

Karak Castle, a fortress of endurance, is more than just a stone structure; it's a living testament to the resilience of the human spirit and the enduring legacy of those who built and protected it. As you stand within its mighty walls and gaze out at the rugged landscape of Jordan, you can't help but feel the weight of history and the echoes of the past that resonate through this remarkable castle.

Umm Qais: Ruins with a View

Nestled in the northernmost part of Jordan, Umm Qais offers visitors a journey through time amidst the backdrop of stunning panoramic views. This archaeological gem, often referred to as the ancient Gadara, is a testament to the rich history of the region and its breathtaking natural beauty.

The Ancient Gadara: Umm Qais was once known as Gadara, a flourishing Greco-Roman city dating back to the Hellenistic period. It was a member of the Decapolis, a league of ten cities in the eastern Roman Empire. Its strategic location on a hill overlooking the Sea of Galilee and the Golan Heights made it a vital center for trade and culture.

Architectural Marvels: The ruins of Gadara at Umm Qais are a testament to the city's architectural prowess. Visitors can explore well-preserved remnants of a theater, basilica, colonnaded streets, and other structures. The ancient theater, in particular, offers an excellent vantage point to appreciate the surrounding landscape.

Spectacular Views: What sets Umm Qais apart is its breathtaking views. Standing at the ancient theater, you can gaze out over the Jordan Valley, the Sea of Galilee, and even glimpse the distant hills of the Golan Heights. The blend of history and nature is awe-inspiring.

Cultural Crossroads: Throughout its history, Gadara was influenced by various civilizations, including the Greeks, Romans, Byzantines, and Arabs. This cultural blend is reflected in the architecture and inscriptions found at the site.

The Gadara Decapolis Museum: Umm Qais is home to the Gadara Decapolis Museum, which houses a collection of artifacts and historical information about the region. It provides valuable insights into the history and significance of Gadara.

A Journey Through Time: Walking through Umm Qais is like stepping back in time. The stone-paved streets, the well-preserved columns, and the remnants of ancient buildings transport you to an era when this city thrived as a cultural and intellectual hub.

A Cultural Hub: Beyond its archaeological significance, Umm Qais is a place where culture thrives. It hosts cultural events, music festivals, and art exhibitions that celebrate the heritage of the region.

An Eclectic Experience: Umm Qais offers an eclectic experience, where history enthusiasts, nature lovers, and photography enthusiasts can all find something to appreciate. It's a place where you can explore the past and savor the beauty of the present.

A Place to Contemplate: As you stand on the ruins of Gadara and gaze out at the sweeping vistas, you can't help but contemplate the passage of time and the enduring allure of this place. It's a site that encourages reflection and appreciation for the historical treasures of Jordan.

Umm Qais, with its ruins and views, is a testament to the enduring legacy of ancient civilizations and the natural beauty of Jordan's northern landscapes. It's a place where history and nature converge, inviting visitors to explore the past while enjoying the breathtaking scenery. Whether you're drawn to archaeology, culture, or simply the joy of discovery, Umm Qais offers a unique and enriching experience that lingers in the memory long after you've left its ancient stones and sweeping vistas behind.

Cultural Mosaic: Jordan's Diverse Population

In the heart of the Middle East, Jordan stands as a diverse and culturally rich nation, defined by the mosaic of its population. The people of Jordan represent a tapestry of traditions, languages, religions, and histories, coming together to form a unique and harmonious society.

The Bedouin Heritage: One of the prominent cultural threads in Jordan is its Bedouin heritage. The Bedouin, traditionally nomadic desert dwellers, have deep-rooted customs that have shaped the country's character. Their hospitality, strong sense of community, and connection to the land continue to influence Jordanian culture.

Arab Identity: The majority of Jordan's population identifies as Arab, sharing linguistic and cultural ties with their fellow Arabs across the region. The Arabic language serves as a unifying force, and it is widely spoken and understood across the country.

Religious Diversity: Religious diversity is a hallmark of Jordan's society. The country is home to a significant Muslim majority, with Sunni Islam being the predominant branch. Additionally, there are Christian communities, including Greek Orthodox, Roman Catholic, and Protestant denominations. Religious coexistence and tolerance are fundamental principles in Jordan, making it a model for harmony in a region often marked by religious divisions.

Christian Holy Sites: Jordan is host to several significant Christian holy sites, such as the baptism site of Jesus Christ at Bethany Beyond the Jordan. These sites attract pilgrims from around the world and serve as a testament to the country's religious diversity.

The Circassian and Chechen Communities: Jordan is also home to Circassian and Chechen communities, who trace their origins to the Caucasus region. They have preserved their unique cultural traditions, and their contributions to Jordan's cultural mosaic are notable.

Urban and Rural Contrasts: Jordan's population is distributed across urban centers, including the capital city of Amman, and rural areas. This diversity in living environments reflects different ways of life, from bustling city life to the tranquility of rural communities.

The Impact of Refugees: Jordan has been a refuge for people fleeing conflicts in neighboring countries, including Palestinians, Iraqis, and Syrians. The presence of these refugee communities has added complexity and depth to Jordan's cultural landscape, emphasizing the nation's commitment to humanitarian values.

Cultural Celebrations: Throughout the year, Jordanians celebrate a variety of cultural festivals and events that reflect their diversity. These celebrations showcase traditional music, dance, and cuisine, offering visitors a chance to immerse themselves in Jordan's vibrant culture.

A Nation United: Despite its diversity, Jordan has successfully cultivated a sense of national unity and identity. This unity is rooted in a shared love for the country, its history, and a commitment to preserving its rich heritage.

The Jordanian Identity: Ultimately, the Jordanian identity is defined by the collective experiences and values of its people. It's a nation where diversity is not a source of division but a strength, where cultural traditions are celebrated, and where the harmonious coexistence of different communities stands as a testament to the power of unity in diversity.

Jordan's cultural mosaic is a reflection of the nation's openness, tolerance, and deep respect for its diverse population. It's a place where history and tradition blend seamlessly with modernity, and where the richness of its culture welcomes all who visit with open arms. Jordan's strength lies in the diversity of its people, and their commitment to preserving their unique traditions while embracing the shared values that bind them together as one nation.

Bedouin Culture: Nomadic Traditions of the Desert

In the vast, arid landscapes of Jordan's deserts, a resilient and enduring culture has thrived for centuries. The Bedouin people, known for their nomadic way of life, have forged a unique heritage deeply intertwined with the unforgiving beauty of the desert. Their traditions, customs, and values are an essential part of Jordan's cultural tapestry.

Nomadic Heritage: The Bedouin way of life is characterized by mobility and adaptability. Traditionally, they roamed the deserts with their herds of camels, goats, and sheep, seeking water and pasture. This nomadic existence demanded a deep knowledge of the desert's secrets, such as finding hidden water sources and navigating the shifting sands.

Tribal Structure: Bedouin society is organized into tribes, each with its own leadership structure and customs. These tribes are a source of identity and provide a sense of belonging for their members. The tribal structure remains a vital aspect of Bedouin culture in modern Jordan.

Hospitality as a Virtue: One of the most cherished values in Bedouin culture is hospitality. A Bedouin will go to great lengths to welcome and provide for guests, as it is considered a sacred duty. Visitors are offered shelter, food, and companionship, often in the form of a communal meal.

The Power of Stories: Oral traditions play a crucial role in preserving Bedouin culture. Stories, songs, and poetry are used to pass down history, wisdom, and the values of the tribe. These stories often revolve around heroic deeds, love, and the challenges of desert life.

The Importance of Camels: Camels are central to Bedouin life, serving as a means of transportation, a source of food, and a symbol of wealth. The camel's ability to endure the harsh desert conditions is highly valued, and the camel holds a revered place in Bedouin culture.

Traditional Attire: Bedouin clothing is both practical and symbolic. The distinctive attire includes flowing robes and headdresses designed to protect against the elements and maintain modesty. The choice of clothing and accessories often indicates a person's tribe and social status.

Music and Dance: Music and dance are integral to Bedouin celebrations and gatherings. Traditional instruments like the rebaba and the mijwiz accompany lively dances, creating an atmosphere of joy and unity.

Challenges and Modernization: While Bedouin culture remains deeply rooted in tradition, it has also adapted to the challenges of the modern world. Many Bedouin now live in settled communities, where they continue to preserve their heritage while engaging in contemporary life.

Tourism and Bedouin Experiences: For visitors to Jordan, experiencing Bedouin culture is an enriching and educational opportunity. Bedouin camps in the desert offer travelers a chance to immerse themselves in traditional customs, taste Bedouin cuisine, and explore the desert with experienced guides.

A Legacy of Resilience: The Bedouin people of Jordan embody resilience, resourcefulness, and a deep connection to the land. Their nomadic traditions are a testament to humanity's ability to adapt and thrive in the harshest of environments. Bedouin culture is not just a relic of the past; it's a living heritage that continues to shape the cultural identity of modern Jordan.

In the heart of the desert, amidst shifting sands and endless horizons, Bedouin culture remains a symbol of resilience and adaptability. The values of hospitality, community, and tradition continue to be cherished by the Bedouin people, who welcome visitors to share in the enduring legacy of their nomadic way of life.

Jordanian Hospitality: A Warm Welcome

In the heart of Jordan, amid the ancient ruins and sprawling landscapes, there exists a tradition deeply embedded in the culture—a tradition as old as the land itself. It's the tradition of hospitality, and in Jordan, it's not merely a gesture; it's a way of life.

A Culture of Generosity: Hospitality in Jordan is not an occasional act; it's a core value that shapes interactions, relationships, and the very essence of daily life. The Jordanian people take immense pride in their reputation for being among the world's most hospitable hosts.

The Welcoming Smile: From the moment you set foot in Jordan, you're met with warm smiles and friendly greetings. Whether you're in bustling Amman or a remote desert village, the genuine and warm hospitality is a constant.

Inviting Strangers In: Jordanians have a saying, "Dawamek ahlamek," which translates to "Your guest is your dream." It reflects the belief that guests are a source of joy and blessings. Jordanians are known to invite strangers into their homes, offering them tea, coffee, and often, a delicious meal.

The Three Cups of Coffee: When you visit a Jordanian home, you're likely to experience the ritual of drinking three cups of coffee. The first cup is strong and bitter, the second is slightly sweeter, and the third is sweet. Each cup represents the stages of a growing relationship, from initial formality to deep friendship.

Feasting as a Form of Love: Food is a central element of Jordanian hospitality. Guests are treated to a feast of traditional dishes, showcasing the rich flavors of Jordanian cuisine. The generosity of the hosts is evident in the abundance and variety of dishes served.

Bedouin Traditions: In the desert, Bedouin communities uphold their own unique traditions of hospitality. Travelers who venture into the desert may find themselves welcomed into a Bedouin tent, where they can share stories, enjoy traditional music, and savor the simple yet flavorful Bedouin cuisine.

The Sacred Duty of Hosts: For Jordanians, being a gracious host is not just a courtesy; it's a sacred duty. There's a strong sense of responsibility to ensure guests feel comfortable and cared for.

A Tapestry of Cultures: Jordan's long history as a crossroads of civilizations has contributed to its rich tapestry of cultural influences. This diversity is reflected in the hospitality traditions, where you may encounter aspects of Arab, Bedouin, and even Circassian hospitality, each with its unique charm.

Tourism and Hospitality: Jordan's growing tourism industry has further amplified its reputation for hospitality. Visitors are welcomed with open arms, and countless hotels, restaurants, and tour operators uphold the country's tradition of warm hospitality.

A Lasting Impression: Jordanian hospitality is not a fleeting experience; it's a memory etched in the hearts of travelers. It's the kindness of strangers, the warmth of newfound friends, and the sense of being truly welcomed in a foreign land.

In Jordan, hospitality is not just a custom; it's an expression of genuine warmth, kindness, and a deep-rooted belief that every guest is a cherished gift. It's an invitation to share in the beauty of the land and the richness of its culture, leaving visitors with a profound sense of connection and a lifelong appreciation for the generosity of the Jordanian people.

Traditional Clothing: From Keffiyeh to Abaya

Traditional clothing in Jordan is a fascinating reflection of the country's rich history, diverse cultural influences, and the practical needs of its people in various regions and climates. From the iconic keffiyeh to the elegant abaya, these garments tell stories of tradition, identity, and adaptation.

The Keffiyeh: Perhaps one of the most recognizable symbols of Jordan and the broader Middle East is the keffiyeh, a square-shaped scarf traditionally worn by Bedouin men. Its distinctive black and white checkered pattern is not merely a fashion statement but also a practical accessory. The keffiyeh provides protection from the scorching sun and blowing desert sands. It can be wrapped around the head or neck, offering shade and relief from the harsh desert environment.

The Ghutrah: The ghutrah is another term for the keffiyeh, used interchangeably in Jordan. While the classic black and white pattern remains the most common, variations in color and design are found across the region, each often associated with specific tribes or communities.

The Bisht: The bisht is a traditional cloak, typically worn over formal attire during special occasions. Made of fine wool, it features intricate embroidery and adds an air of dignity and elegance to the wearer. The bisht is commonly worn by men, especially during weddings and important ceremonies.

The Dishdasha: The dishdasha, also known as the thobe or kandura in different parts of the Arab world, is a long robe worn by men. In Jordan, it's typically ankle-length and made of lightweight fabric to combat the desert heat. The dishdasha is practical and comfortable attire, suitable for daily wear.

The Abaya: For women in Jordan, the abaya is a common traditional garment. This full-length robe is often black and worn over regular clothing. It serves both cultural and religious purposes, providing modesty and a sense of identity. In urban areas, the abaya may be more colorful or adorned with embroidery.

Cultural Significance: Traditional clothing in Jordan carries deep cultural significance. It reflects the wearer's connection to their heritage, whether they are Bedouin, urban, or rural Jordanians. The choice of attire can also signify one's social status or profession.

Adaptation to Modern Life: While traditional clothing remains an essential part of Jordanian culture, it has also adapted to modern life. In cities like Amman, you'll find a blend of traditional attire and Western clothing, reflecting the dynamic nature of Jordanian society.

Preserving Heritage: Efforts to preserve and promote traditional clothing continue in Jordan. Artisans and designers are working to ensure that these garments continue to be valued and celebrated in the modern world.

Traditional clothing in Jordan is not just about fashion; it's a living expression of heritage, identity, and adaptation to the environment. Whether it's the practical keffiyeh worn by Bedouin in the desert, the elegant bisht donned for special occasions, or the abaya that signifies modesty and tradition for women, these garments are a testament to the enduring cultural richness of Jordan. In a world of constant change, they remain a source of pride and a link to the country's timeless past.

Music and Dance: The Rhythms of Jordan

In the heart of Jordan, amidst its ancient landscapes and rich cultural tapestry, music and dance echo through the ages, forming an essential part of the nation's identity. These rhythms are not merely entertainment; they are expressions of heritage, community, and the enduring spirit of the Jordanian people.

Traditional Jordanian Music: Jordan boasts a diverse range of musical traditions, influenced by its Bedouin, Arab, and Circassian communities. Traditional Jordanian music often features instruments like the oud (a stringed instrument similar to a lute), the rebaba (a type of fiddle), and the mijwiz (a double-reeded instrument). These instruments come together to create soul-stirring melodies that have been passed down through generations.

The Dabkeh: If there's one dance that embodies Jordanian culture, it's the dabkeh. This lively and energetic dance is performed in a group, with dancers holding hands and forming a line or a circle. The synchronized stomping of feet to the beat of the music is not only a display of skill but also a symbol of unity and community.

Bedouin Music: The Bedouin communities of Jordan have their own unique musical traditions. Bedouin songs, often accompanied by instruments like the rababa and the rebaba, tell stories of desert life, honor tribal heritage, and convey the deep connection between the Bedouin people and their harsh yet beautiful environment.

Influences from the Arab World: Jordan's proximity to other Arab nations has allowed for the exchange of musical influences. You can hear echoes of Egyptian, Syrian, and Lebanese music in Jordanian compositions. This cultural fusion has resulted in a rich and dynamic musical landscape.

Contemporary Music: Jordan's contemporary music scene is vibrant and diverse. Modern genres like pop, rock, and hip-hop have found a place in the hearts of young Jordanians. Local artists often blend traditional elements with contemporary sounds, creating music that reflects the evolving nature of Jordanian society.

Cultural Celebrations: Music and dance take center stage during Jordan's cultural celebrations and festivals. Events like the Jerash Festival and the Jordan Festival showcase traditional and contemporary performances, attracting both local and international audiences.

Preservation of Heritage: Efforts are underway to preserve and promote Jordan's musical heritage. Cultural institutions and organizations work to ensure that traditional songs and dances are passed on to future generations, keeping the flame of Jordanian culture burning brightly.

Tourism and Cultural Experiences: For visitors to Jordan, experiencing the country's music and dance is a captivating journey. You can witness live performances in vibrant cities like Amman, or you can immerse yourself in the heart of Jordan's musical traditions by participating in Bedouin celebrations in the desert.

Music and dance in Jordan are more than just artistic expressions; they are living traditions that connect people to their roots, foster community bonds, and tell the stories of a nation. They are the rhythms of Jordan, resonating through time and space, inviting all who listen and watch to become part of the country's vibrant cultural narrative.

Jordanian Artistry: Calligraphy and Craftsmanship

In the heart of Jordan, artistry flourishes in the form of calligraphy and craftsmanship, weaving a tapestry of culture and creativity that reflects the nation's rich heritage. These artistic traditions are not just about aesthetics; they are expressions of identity, spirituality, and the timeless beauty of the Arabic script.

The Art of Calligraphy: Calligraphy, the art of beautiful writing, holds a special place in Jordanian culture. The Arabic script itself is a work of art, characterized by its flowing, cursive lines. Calligraphers in Jordan master various styles, from the classical to the contemporary, each offering a unique perspective on the written word.

The Quranic Connection: Calligraphy has deep spiritual significance in Jordan. Many calligraphic works feature verses from the Quran, showcasing the reverence and respect that Jordanians hold for their religious texts. The intricate calligraphy adorning mosques and religious buildings is a testament to the divine beauty of the Arabic script.

Traditional Crafts: Craftsmanship in Jordan is a labor of love, with artisans producing a wide range of traditional items, from pottery and ceramics to textiles and jewelry. Each piece is a testament to the skill and dedication of the craftsmen and women who carry on these age-old traditions.

Mosaics and Pottery: The art of mosaic-making has a long history in Jordan. The city of Madaba, often called the "City of Mosaics," is famous for its stunning mosaic floors that depict intricate scenes from history and mythology. Jordanian pottery is also renowned for its quality and craftsmanship, with traditional designs passed down through generations.

Contemporary Expression: Jordan's art scene is not confined to tradition; it also embraces contemporary forms of expression. Modern artists in Jordan draw inspiration from their rich cultural heritage while exploring new mediums and techniques. Galleries in cities like Amman showcase a diverse range of artistic talents.

Preservation of Heritage: Efforts to preserve and promote Jordanian artistry are ongoing. Cultural institutions and organizations work tirelessly to ensure that these traditions continue to thrive. Workshops and programs are held to educate the younger generation about the importance of preserving their artistic heritage.

Tourism and Cultural Immersion: For travelers to Jordan, experiencing the country's artistry is a captivating journey. Visitors can explore museums and galleries, visit workshops to witness artisans at work, and even participate in hands-on activities to create their own crafts.

Jordanian artistry is more than just a visual feast; it's a profound connection to the past, a celebration of the present, and a bridge to the future. Whether it's the mesmerizing calligraphy that graces the walls of mosques, the intricate mosaics that tell stories of bygone eras, or the skilled craftsmanship that produces exquisite pottery and textiles, these artistic traditions are a testament to the enduring creativity and cultural richness of Jordan. They are the expressions of a nation, a reflection of its soul, and a source of inspiration for generations to come.

Religion in Jordan: A Tolerance and Faith

Religion in Jordan is a profound and multifaceted aspect of the nation's identity. The Hashemite Kingdom of Jordan is known for its deep commitment to religious tolerance and coexistence, making it a unique example in the Middle East where people of various faiths peacefully share the same land.

Islamic Heritage: The majority of Jordanians are Muslims, with Sunni Islam being the predominant branch. The Hashemite monarchy, which has ruled Jordan since its establishment, holds a special status in the Islamic world as descendants of the Prophet Muhammad. This lineage has earned Jordan the title of the "Hashemite Kingdom."

Religious Freedom: Jordan's constitution guarantees freedom of religion, and the country is known for its welcoming stance towards religious minorities. The government recognizes and respects the rights of various religious communities, including Christians, Druze, and others.

Christian Communities: Jordan is home to a significant Christian population, with various denominations such as Greek Orthodox, Roman Catholic, and Protestant. Historical religious sites, including those associated with biblical events, draw pilgrims and tourists alike.

Religious Sites: Jordan is blessed with numerous religious sites of historical and spiritual significance. The Baptism

Site (Bethany Beyond the Jordan) is believed to be where Jesus was baptized by John the Baptist. Mount Nebo, where Moses is said to have seen the Promised Land before his death, is another revered location.

Religious Festivals: Jordanians celebrate religious festivals with fervor and joy. Eid al-Fitr, marking the end of Ramadan, and Eid al-Adha, the Feast of Sacrifice, are two major Islamic celebrations. Christmas is widely observed by the Christian community, with various traditions and events.

Interfaith Harmony: Jordan promotes interfaith dialogue and cooperation, fostering understanding and tolerance among religious communities. The Amman Message, an initiative that seeks to clarify the true teachings of Islam, was launched in Jordan and has garnered global recognition.

Protection of Holy Sites: Jordan is entrusted with the protection and maintenance of numerous holy sites. The government invests in preserving and conserving these places, recognizing their significance to not only the nation but also to the global religious community.

Religious Tourism: Jordan's religious heritage is a major draw for religious tourists and pilgrims from around the world. Visitors are welcomed to explore the country's sacred sites and experience the warm hospitality of the Jordanian people.

Faith and Identity: Religion plays a central role in the lives of Jordanians, shaping their values, customs, and sense of identity. It's not just a matter of personal belief; it's a fundamental part of the nation's collective consciousness.

In Jordan, religion is not a source of division but a unifying force that brings people together in mutual respect and understanding. It's a testament to the country's commitment to harmony and coexistence, where faith is not a barrier but a bridge to building a diverse and united society. Jordan's approach to religion sets a remarkable example in a region often characterized by religious strife, showing that tolerance and faith can indeed coexist harmoniously.

Festivals and Celebrations: Jordan's Joyous Occasions

In Jordan, the calendar is marked not only by the passage of time but also by a tapestry of vibrant festivals and celebrations. These joyous occasions offer a glimpse into the rich cultural tapestry of the nation, where traditions, customs, and merriment come together in splendid harmony.

Eid al-Fitr: One of the most important festivals in Jordan and the Islamic world, Eid al-Fitr marks the end of Ramadan, the holy month of fasting. Families come together to celebrate with special prayers, feasts, and the exchange of gifts. It's a time of forgiveness, gratitude, and communal bonding.

Eid al-Adha: Known as the Feast of Sacrifice, this Eid commemorates Abraham's willingness to sacrifice his son, an act of obedience to God. Families gather to offer prayers, share meals, and distribute meat to the less fortunate. It's a time of compassion and giving.

Christmas: Jordan's Christian population celebrates Christmas with great fervor. The streets are adorned with colorful decorations, and churches host midnight Mass services. Nativity scenes and traditional carols are an integral part of the festivities.

Prophet Mohammad's Birthday: The birth of the Prophet Mohammad is celebrated with religious fervor. Mosques are illuminated, and special prayers and recitations from the

Quran are held. The occasion emphasizes the importance of the Prophet's teachings in Islamic life.

Independence Day: On May 25th, Jordanians celebrate their independence from British mandate rule in 1946. Festivities include parades, cultural performances, and the display of the Jordanian flag. It's a day of national pride and unity.

New Year's Eve: As the world bids farewell to one year and welcomes another, Jordanians join in the global celebration. Cities like Amman come alive with fireworks, parties, and festivities, creating a lively atmosphere.

Arab Renaissance Day: Celebrated on February 8th, Arab Renaissance Day honors the Arab heritage and contributions to culture, science, and knowledge. It's a day to reflect on the achievements of the Arab world.

Cultural Festivals: Jordan hosts various cultural festivals throughout the year, showcasing music, dance, theater, and arts. The Jerash Festival, held in the ancient city of Jerash, is a prominent event featuring performances from local and international artists.

Food Festivals: Jordan's culinary traditions are celebrated in food festivals like the Jordan Food Week, where locals and tourists can savor a wide array of traditional and modern Jordanian dishes.

Desert Festivals: In the vast desert landscapes of Jordan, events like the Wadi Rum Desert Challenge attract adventure enthusiasts from around the world. It's a thrilling celebration of desert sports and exploration.

Film Festivals: Jordan's film industry is gaining recognition, and events like the Amman International Film Festival provide a platform for local and international filmmakers to showcase their work.

These festivals and celebrations in Jordan are not just moments on the calendar but reflections of the nation's diverse cultural heritage and its commitment to fostering unity and joy. Whether religious or secular, they bring people together in a spirit of harmony and celebration, showcasing the enduring traditions and vibrant soul of Jordan.

Education in Jordan: Nurturing Minds for the Future

Education in Jordan is a cornerstone of the nation's development and progress. With a strong commitment to nurturing minds for the future, Jordan has made significant strides in providing quality education to its citizens. Here, knowledge is seen as a vital resource, and investments in education reflect the nation's dedication to empowering its youth and preparing them for the challenges and opportunities of the modern world.

Basic Education: Jordan ensures that every child has access to primary and secondary education. The Ministry of Education oversees the public education system, which is free and compulsory for children aged 6 to 16. This foundation equips students with essential skills and knowledge.

Gender Equality: Jordan has made commendable progress in promoting gender equality in education. Both girls and boys have equal access to educational opportunities, and the gender gap in literacy rates has significantly decreased over the years.

Tertiary Education: Jordan boasts a growing number of universities and colleges offering a wide range of academic programs. The country's flagship institution, the University of Jordan, is renowned for its research and academic excellence. Other universities and institutions provide diverse fields of study, catering to the diverse interests of students.

Technical and Vocational Training: Jordan recognizes the importance of technical and vocational education in preparing students for the workforce. Various vocational training centers and programs are available to equip individuals with practical skills, enhancing their employability.

Private Education: In addition to public institutions, private schools and universities play a crucial role in the education landscape. They offer a choice for parents and students seeking alternative educational paths.

Multilingualism: Jordan's education system emphasizes multilingualism. Arabic is the primary language of instruction, but English is widely taught as a second language, preparing students for global communication and collaboration.

Higher Education Opportunities Abroad: Jordanian students are encouraged to pursue higher education opportunities abroad, with scholarships and exchange programs available to support their academic journeys.

Education Reforms: The Jordanian government continues to invest in education reforms aimed at improving the quality of education. Initiatives include curriculum enhancements, teacher training, and the integration of technology into classrooms.

Youth Empowerment: Jordan recognizes the potential of its youth as agents of change. Youth empowerment programs and initiatives focus on leadership development, entrepreneurship, and civic engagement, allowing young people to contribute to the nation's growth.

Challenges: While Jordan has made significant strides in education, challenges remain. These include addressing overcrowded classrooms, ensuring quality education in underserved areas, and aligning educational outcomes with the demands of the job market.

Education in Jordan is not just about imparting knowledge; it's about shaping the future of the nation. It's a testament to Jordan's commitment to progress and development, with education serving as the bridge to a brighter tomorrow. As Jordan continues to invest in its educational infrastructure and the intellectual development of its youth, it stands poised to meet the challenges and opportunities of the ever-evolving global landscape.

Jordan's Economy: A Growing Hub in the Region

Jordan's economy is a dynamic and growing hub in the Middle East, characterized by resilience, diversification, and a commitment to progress. Situated in a region often marked by economic challenges and political instability, Jordan has charted a path of economic development that positions it as a key player on the global stage.

Economic Stability: Jordan's prudent fiscal policies and financial reforms have contributed to its economic stability. The country has managed to weather regional and global economic fluctuations, maintaining a relatively low inflation rate and a stable currency.

Diversification: The Jordanian government has made significant efforts to diversify the economy. While historically reliant on industries like phosphate mining and agriculture, Jordan has expanded into sectors such as manufacturing, tourism, information technology, and renewable energy.

Free Trade Agreements: Jordan has entered into various free trade agreements with countries around the world, including the United States and the European Union. These agreements have facilitated access to international markets, boosting exports and foreign investment.

Tourism: Jordan's rich historical and cultural heritage, including iconic sites like Petra and the Dead Sea, make it a prime destination for tourists. The tourism sector has seen steady growth, contributing significantly to the country's GDP.

Foreign Investment: Jordan has actively sought foreign investment, offering incentives and a business-friendly environment to attract capital. As a result, foreign direct investment has flowed into sectors such as manufacturing, real estate, and technology.

Information Technology: Jordan has emerged as a regional hub for information technology and outsourcing services. The country's well-educated workforce and modern infrastructure have made it an attractive destination for tech companies.

Renewable Energy: With limited natural resources, Jordan has turned to renewable energy sources to meet its power needs. The nation has invested in solar and wind energy projects, reducing reliance on imported fossil fuels.

Youth Employment: Jordan recognizes the importance of youth employment and entrepreneurship. Initiatives to empower young people and support startups are contributing to a vibrant entrepreneurial ecosystem.

Challenges: Despite its achievements, Jordan faces economic challenges. These include a high unemployment rate, particularly among youth, and the need for further reforms to enhance the business environment.

Resilience: Jordan's economy has shown resilience in the face of regional instability. The government's commitment to economic development and diversification has played a crucial role in maintaining stability.

Global Integration: Jordan's strategic location and its openness to trade have positioned it as a key player in regional and global economic networks. The country continues to explore opportunities for economic integration and cooperation.

Jordan's economy is a testament to its determination to overcome challenges and pursue sustainable growth. As the nation continues to invest in diversification, innovation, and human capital, it remains a dynamic economic hub in the Middle East, poised to seize new opportunities and contribute to regional stability and prosperity.

Jordanian Royalty: A Modern Monarchy

Jordanian royalty stands as a symbol of continuity, stability, and unity in the Hashemite Kingdom of Jordan. Rooted in centuries of tradition and history, the modern monarchy in Jordan plays a significant role in the country's governance and identity.

The Hashemite Dynasty: Jordan's monarchy belongs to the Hashemite dynasty, tracing its lineage back to the Prophet Muhammad. The Hashemite family has played a prominent role in the Arab world, and this historical legacy has contributed to its legitimacy as the ruling family in Jordan.

King Abdullah II: The current monarch, King Abdullah II, ascended to the throne in 1999 after the passing of his father, King Hussein. King Abdullah II is widely respected for his leadership and efforts to modernize the country. He has focused on political and economic reforms, as well as diplomacy in the region.

Queen Rania: Queen Rania, the wife of King Abdullah II, is known for her advocacy work on various social issues, including education, women's rights, and youth empowerment. Her international presence has also raised the profile of Jordan on the global stage.

Royal Institutions: The Hashemite monarchy in Jordan operates within a constitutional framework that includes the parliament and the judiciary. While the king holds executive authority, Jordan has made strides toward greater political pluralism.

Stability and Unity: The monarchy has played a crucial role in maintaining stability and national unity, especially during challenging times in the region. Jordan's ability to navigate regional conflicts and maintain peaceful relations with neighboring countries is, in part, attributed to its monarchy.

Modernization and Reform: King Abdullah II has championed modernization and reform efforts in Jordan, seeking to enhance economic development, governance, and democratic institutions. The monarchy's commitment to these reforms has been a defining feature of its rule.

Diplomatic Role: Jordan's monarchy has also played a diplomatic role in the region, advocating for peace and stability. Jordan has been a key player in peace negotiations in the Middle East, including its role in the Israel-Jordan peace treaty of 1994.

Cultural Significance: The monarchy holds cultural significance for Jordanians, serving as a unifying force in the country. The royal family participates in various cultural and national events, further cementing its connection with the people.

Challenges and Opportunities: While Jordan's monarchy has contributed to the nation's stability and development, it faces challenges, including economic reforms, political reforms, and youth unemployment. However, the monarchy remains committed to addressing these challenges.

In Jordan, the monarchy is not just a historical relic but a contemporary institution that plays a pivotal role in the nation's governance and identity. Rooted in tradition yet forward-looking, the Jordanian monarchy continues to adapt and evolve, seeking to meet the aspirations of its people and contribute to regional stability in an ever-changing world.

Arabic Language: Communication and Expression

The Arabic language is a tapestry woven with history, culture, and tradition, serving as a vibrant thread that ties together the diverse nations and peoples of the Arab world. It is a language of eloquence and expression, a medium through which poetry, literature, and daily communication flow seamlessly.

Historical Significance: Arabic is not just a language; it's a historical treasure. It traces its roots back to the Arabian Peninsula, where it evolved over centuries. The Quran, the holy book of Islam, is written in Classical Arabic, and this sacred text has played a pivotal role in shaping the language.

Language of Poetry: Arabic is renowned for its poetic richness. Arabic poetry is a beloved art form, with poets crafting intricate verses that explore themes of love, nature, and the human condition. The language's complex grammar and vocabulary provide a canvas for poetic expression.

Literary Legacy: Arabic literature is a treasure trove of stories, from the epic tales of "One Thousand and One Nights" to the philosophical works of scholars like Ibn Sina (Avicenna) and Ibn Rushd (Averroes). The Arabic literary tradition has influenced writers and thinkers worldwide.

Modern Standard Arabic: While Classical Arabic is revered for its literary and religious significance, Modern Standard Arabic (MSA) serves as a lingua franca in the Arab world. MSA is used in formal contexts, including education, media, and government.

Dialects: Arabic is a language of dialects, with each Arab country and region having its own unique spoken variety. These dialects often differ significantly from MSA, both in pronunciation and vocabulary. Jordan, for example, has its own distinct Jordanian Arabic dialect.

Cultural Identity: The Arabic language is a cornerstone of cultural identity in the Arab world. It is a source of pride and unity among Arabs, transcending national boundaries.

Calligraphy: Arabic calligraphy is an art form in its own right, with intricate and beautiful script styles. Calligraphy artists skillfully craft Arabic letters into visual masterpieces, often used to decorate mosques, manuscripts, and buildings.

Language of Islam: Arabic is the language of Islam, and Muslims around the world recite Quranic verses and perform prayers in Arabic. This linguistic connection to the religion adds to the language's significance.

Challenges and Opportunities: Despite its rich heritage, Arabic faces challenges in the modern world, including the need to adapt to the demands of technology and globalization. Efforts to promote Arabic education and preserve its linguistic heritage are ongoing.

Arabic is not just a language; it's a cultural treasure that binds together diverse nations and peoples. It's a language of expression, eloquence, and profound historical significance. Whether in the verses of poetry or the teachings of the Quran, Arabic continues to shape the hearts and minds of millions, serving as a bridge between tradition and modernity.

Arabic Script: The Beauty of Calligraphy

The Arabic script is a work of art in itself, a symphony of lines and curves that come together to create one of the world's most beautiful and distinctive writing systems. It's a script that carries not just words but also a sense of history, culture, and aesthetics.

Historical Roots: The roots of the Arabic script date back to the 4th century CE when it emerged in the Arabian Peninsula. Its early forms were cursive, and it evolved over time to the script we know today.

Cursive Elegance: Arabic calligraphy is known for its cursive elegance. Each letter flows seamlessly into the next, creating a harmonious and visually pleasing composition. The letters are interconnected, with initial, medial, and final forms, adding complexity and beauty to the script.

Artistic Expressiveness: Calligraphy in Arabic is an art form, and calligraphers are revered for their skill and creativity. They use various script styles, such as Naskh, Thuluth, Diwani, and Nastaliq, to create intricate and visually stunning compositions.

Sacred Significance: The Arabic script is deeply intertwined with Islam, as it is the script in which the Quran, the holy book of Islam, is written. The Quranic calligraphy is a revered art form and is often used to decorate mosques and religious texts.

Versatility: Arabic calligraphy is versatile and adaptable. It can be found in various forms of artistic expression, from decorative inscriptions on buildings and monuments to ornate Quranic manuscripts. It has also been integrated into modern design and branding.

International Influence: Arabic calligraphy has had a significant influence on other scripts and cultures. For example, it played a role in the development of the Persian script, and its artistic elements have inspired artists worldwide.

Education and Preservation: Efforts to preserve and promote Arabic calligraphy are ongoing. Calligraphy schools and workshops exist in many Arab countries, passing on this ancient art form to new generations.

Global Appreciation: The beauty of Arabic calligraphy transcends linguistic and cultural boundaries. It is admired by people of various backgrounds for its aesthetic qualities.

Challenges: While Arabic calligraphy thrives in many ways, it faces challenges, particularly in the digital age. The shift to digital writing and printing has raised concerns about the preservation of traditional calligraphy skills.

The Arabic script is not just a tool for writing; it's a testament to human creativity and expression. It carries the weight of history and culture while continuing to evolve and inspire. Whether adorning the walls of a mosque or the cover of a book, Arabic calligraphy is a timeless art that speaks to the soul with its beauty and elegance.

Learning Arabic: A Beginner's Guide

Learning Arabic, a language of rich history and cultural significance, can be a rewarding endeavor for beginners. While it's true that Arabic may appear challenging at first due to its unique script and complex grammar, with determination and the right approach, anyone can embark on this linguistic journey.

The Arabic Alphabet: Arabic is written from right to left, and it uses a script known as the Arabic alphabet. The alphabet consists of 28 letters, and it's essential to learn both the script and the sounds associated with each letter.

Pronunciation: Arabic pronunciation can be different from what English speakers are accustomed to. Pay close attention to sounds like "ع" (ayn) and "ح" (haa), which have no direct equivalent in English.

Basic Vocabulary: Begin with essential vocabulary words and phrases. Greetings like "مرحبًا" (marhaban) for "hello" and "شكرًا" (shukran) for "thank you" are a good starting point.

Grammar: Arabic grammar is intricate, with features like verb conjugations and noun cases. Start with the basics, such as understanding the three cases: nominative, accusative, and genitive.

Tenses: Arabic verbs are conjugated according to tense, person, and gender. The most basic tenses to learn are the past, present, and future.

Arabic Dialects: Keep in mind that spoken Arabic varies across regions. While Modern Standard Arabic (MSA) is used for formal contexts, each Arab country has its own dialect for everyday conversation. Learning a specific dialect may be helpful if you plan to live or travel in a particular region.

Resources: Invest in language learning resources like textbooks, online courses, and language apps. Joining Arabic classes or finding a language partner can also provide valuable support.

Practice: Consistent practice is key to language learning. Dedicate time each day to reading, writing, listening, and speaking in Arabic. Immerse yourself in the language as much as possible.

Cultural Immersion: Understanding Arabic culture can enhance your language learning experience. Explore Arabic music, films, and literature to gain insight into the culture and context of the language.

Patience and Persistence: Learning any language takes time, and Arabic is no exception. Be patient with yourself and stay persistent. Mistakes are a natural part of the learning process.

Language Schools: Consider enrolling in a language school or program that specializes in teaching Arabic. These programs often offer immersive experiences and expert guidance.

Online Communities: Join online communities or forums where learners can connect, share experiences, and seek advice. It's a great way to stay motivated and get answers to your questions.

Learning Arabic is a journey that opens doors to a rich and diverse culture. It's a language of literature, history, and tradition. With dedication, the right resources, and a passion for discovery, beginners can unlock the beauty and depth of the Arabic language. So, embrace this journey, and let your curiosity guide you as you explore the world of Arabic.

Daily Life in Jordan: Customs and Etiquette

Understanding the customs and etiquette of daily life in Jordan is essential for anyone looking to immerse themselves in this beautiful country's culture. Jordanians are known for their warm hospitality, but it's also important to be respectful of their traditions and way of life. Here, we'll delve into the customs and etiquette that shape daily interactions in Jordan.

Hospitality: Jordanians take pride in their hospitality. If you're invited into someone's home, it's customary to bring a small gift, like sweets or fruits, to show your appreciation. Expect to be offered tea or coffee upon arrival, and it's polite to accept.

Greetings: Greetings are an essential part of Jordanian culture. Handshakes are common between men, while women often greet each other with hugs and kisses on both cheeks. When addressing someone, use their title or honorific, such as "Mr." or "Mrs.," followed by their first name.

Conservative Dress: Dress modestly, especially in public places and religious sites. Both men and women should avoid wearing revealing clothing. Women may consider covering their shoulders and knees when in public.

Respect for Religion: Jordan is predominantly Muslim, and Islam plays a significant role in daily life. Show respect for religious customs by not entering mosques if you're not

Muslim, and always remove your shoes before entering someone's home.

Friday is Holy: Friday is considered a holy day in Islam, so many businesses, government offices, and markets may close for part of the day. Plan accordingly when scheduling activities.

Dining Etiquette: When dining in Jordan, it's common to eat with your right hand, as the left hand is traditionally reserved for personal hygiene. Wait for the host to begin the meal or offer a blessing before you start eating.

Sharing Food: If you're invited to a Jordanian home, expect to be served generous portions of delicious dishes. It's considered polite to try a bit of everything and express your appreciation for the meal.

Tipping: Tipping is customary in restaurants, and a service charge may not be included. Leaving a tip of around 10% is appreciated. Tipping for other services, such as taxi rides, is also common.

Language: While Arabic is the official language, many Jordanians, especially in urban areas, speak English. Learning a few basic Arabic phrases can be helpful and is often appreciated.

Public Behavior: Public displays of affection should be kept to a minimum. It's important to be respectful and considerate of local customs, which can be more conservative than in some Western countries.

Gift-Giving: If you receive a gift, it's polite to open it in private rather than in front of the giver. Express gratitude and appreciation for the gesture.

Time: Jordanians have a more relaxed sense of time, so punctuality, while appreciated, is not always strictly adhered to. Be patient and flexible in your scheduling.

By embracing these customs and etiquette, you'll not only show respect for Jordanian culture but also enhance your own experience while exploring this diverse and welcoming country. Jordanians are known for their friendliness and will likely appreciate your efforts to embrace their way of life.

Traveling in Jordan: Tips for a Memorable Visit

Traveling in Jordan offers a captivating journey through a land of history, culture, and natural beauty. To make your visit truly memorable, it's essential to be well-prepared and informed. Here, you'll find valuable tips and insights to ensure you have an unforgettable experience in this remarkable country.

1. Visa Requirements: Check the visa requirements for your nationality before traveling to Jordan. Depending on your country of origin, you may need to obtain a visa in advance or obtain one upon arrival.

2. Currency: The official currency of Jordan is the Jordanian Dinar (JOD). It's advisable to exchange some currency at the airport or a local bank upon arrival for convenience.

3. Language: While Arabic is the official language, English is widely spoken, especially in tourist areas. Learning a few basic Arabic phrases can be helpful and is often appreciated by locals.

4. Local Cuisine: Jordanian cuisine is a delight for the senses. Don't miss the opportunity to savor traditional dishes like falafel, shawarma, and mansaf. Also, indulge in sweet treats like baklava and knafeh.

5. Hydration: The Jordanian climate can be hot and dry, so staying hydrated is crucial, especially if you're exploring desert regions. Carry a reusable water bottle and refill it as needed.

6. Dress Code: Dress modestly, particularly when visiting religious sites or conservative areas. Both men and women should avoid wearing revealing clothing.

7. Respect for Culture: Be respectful of local customs and traditions, especially in rural areas. Ask for permission before taking photos of people, and avoid photographing military or government buildings.

8. Bargaining: Bargaining is common in Jordan's markets and souks. Be prepared to negotiate when shopping for souvenirs or goods, but do so with respect and a friendly attitude.

9. Transportation: Jordan has a reliable and affordable transportation system. Taxis and ride-sharing services are readily available in cities, and buses connect major tourist destinations.

10. Jordan Pass: Consider purchasing the Jordan Pass, which includes entry to many of the country's historical sites and attractions, including Petra. It can save you money and time.

11. Safety: Jordan is generally safe for tourists. Exercise common sense precautions, like safeguarding your belongings and avoiding risky areas, to ensure a worry-free trip.

12. Petra: Petra is one of Jordan's most iconic attractions. Plan to spend a full day exploring this ancient city carved into rose-red cliffs. Start early to avoid crowds and the midday heat.

13. Wadi Rum: Wadi Rum's desert landscape is awe-inspiring. Consider a desert tour or camping experience to fully appreciate its beauty.

14. Dead Sea: Floating in the Dead Sea is a unique experience. Don't forget to bring swimwear and be cautious not to get water in your eyes.

15. Local Interactions: Engage with locals whenever possible. Jordanians are known for their warmth and hospitality, and striking up conversations can lead to memorable cultural exchanges.

16. Travel Insurance: Ensure you have comprehensive travel insurance that covers medical emergencies and trip cancellations. It's a safety net that can provide peace of mind.

17. Jordanian Traditions: Familiarize yourself with Jordanian customs and etiquette, such as removing your shoes before entering someone's home and using your right hand for eating.

18. Time Zone: Jordan operates on Eastern European Time (EET). Make sure to adjust your watches and devices accordingly.

19. Weather: Check the weather forecast for your travel dates and pack accordingly. Jordan can experience extreme temperatures, so bring appropriate clothing and sunscreen.

20. Explore Beyond Tourist Spots: While Petra and the Dead Sea are must-visit places, consider exploring off-the-beaten-path destinations to experience the authentic culture of Jordan.

By keeping these tips in mind and immersing yourself in the local culture, you'll create lasting memories and have a truly remarkable visit to Jordan. This diverse and welcoming country has much to offer the intrepid traveler, from ancient wonders to warm hospitality. Enjoy every moment of your adventure in the heart of the Middle East.

Preserving Jordan's Heritage: Conservation Efforts

Preserving Jordan's heritage is a noble endeavor that encompasses a rich tapestry of history, culture, and natural wonders. Throughout this ancient land, efforts to conserve and protect these treasures are both significant and ongoing. This chapter explores the various conservation initiatives in Jordan, highlighting the commitment to safeguarding its heritage for future generations.

1. Petra Conservation: Petra, Jordan's crown jewel, is a UNESCO World Heritage Site. Extensive efforts have been made to protect its fragile rock-cut architecture and intricate carvings. Conservationists work tirelessly to mitigate erosion, stabilize structures, and preserve this marvel of ancient engineering.

2. Archaeological Sites: Jordan boasts numerous archaeological sites, each with its own unique challenges. Conservationists employ modern techniques to excavate and preserve historical artifacts, revealing insights into the region's deep history.

3. Eco-Tourism: Jordan has embraced eco-tourism as a means of preserving natural landscapes. Protected areas like the Dana Biosphere Reserve and Wadi Rum focus on sustainable tourism practices that benefit local communities while safeguarding the environment.

4. Museum Conservation: Jordan's museums house priceless artifacts, from the Dead Sea Scrolls to ancient pottery. Preservation efforts ensure that these treasures remain in excellent condition, allowing visitors to appreciate their historical significance.

5. Cultural Heritage: Jordan's rich cultural heritage extends beyond archaeological sites. Traditional crafts, such as mosaic art and calligraphy, are passed down through generations, preserving skills and cultural identity.

6. Environmental Conservation: Jordan faces environmental challenges, including water scarcity and desertification. Conservation efforts involve reforestation, water management, and sustainable agriculture practices to protect the country's delicate ecosystem.

7. Wildlife Conservation: The Royal Society for the Conservation of Nature (RSCN) plays a vital role in preserving Jordan's wildlife. Protected areas like Azraq Wetland Reserve provide sanctuary for endangered species like the Arabian Oryx and Syrian wolf.

8. Legal Framework: Jordan has established legal frameworks to protect its heritage. Laws govern the excavation and export of antiquities, ensuring they remain within the country for study and display.

9. Community Involvement: Engaging local communities in conservation efforts is essential. Initiatives like home-stay programs allow travelers to connect with Jordanian families, providing economic benefits to these communities while promoting cultural exchange.

10. Education and Awareness: Educational programs and awareness campaigns inform Jordanians and tourists about the importance of preserving heritage. These initiatives instill a sense of pride and responsibility in safeguarding their nation's treasures.

11. UNESCO Collaboration: Jordan collaborates closely with UNESCO to safeguard its cultural and natural heritage. Joint projects focus on restoration, capacity building, and documentation of heritage sites.

12. Challenges and Future Prospects: Challenges persist, including urbanization, climate change, and illegal excavation. However, Jordan's commitment to preserving its heritage remains strong, with a vision of maintaining its unique identity for generations to come.

The efforts to preserve Jordan's heritage are multifaceted and interconnected, driven by a deep appreciation for the country's historical, cultural, and environmental significance. These conservation endeavors not only protect tangible treasures but also enrich the nation's identity and contribute to a sustainable future. Jordan stands as a testament to the harmonious coexistence of the past and the present, where heritage is revered, celebrated, and conserved with unwavering dedication.

Challenges and Opportunities: Jordan's Future

As we explore the challenges and opportunities that lie ahead for Jordan, we delve into a complex and dynamic landscape. Jordan has always been a nation that has faced its challenges with resilience, and it continues to do so in the present day. Simultaneously, it embraces the opportunities that arise in a rapidly changing world.

1. Geopolitical Challenges: Jordan occupies a strategic position in a region marked by instability. It shares borders with Israel, Syria, Iraq, and Saudi Arabia, which have all experienced political turmoil. Maintaining stability in this context is a constant challenge.

2. Water Scarcity: Jordan is one of the world's most water-scarce countries. The scarcity of this vital resource poses significant challenges for agriculture, industry, and daily life. The country has implemented innovative water management strategies but still faces an ongoing struggle to meet its water needs.

3. Economic Diversification: Jordan's economy is heavily reliant on industries like phosphate mining and tourism. Diversifying the economy to reduce vulnerability to external shocks is an ongoing goal.

4. Refugee Crisis: Jordan has been a refuge for millions of displaced people, including Palestinian refugees and those fleeing the conflict in Syria. Hosting such a large refugee population places significant economic and social burdens on the country.

5. Youth Unemployment: Like many countries in the Middle East, Jordan faces the challenge of high youth unemployment. Creating opportunities for the younger generation is vital for the nation's stability and growth.

6. Education and Innovation: Jordan recognizes the importance of investing in education and fostering innovation to compete in the global economy. The country has made strides in these areas, with universities and research centers driving progress.

7. Environmental Conservation: Jordan is acutely aware of its environmental challenges, from desertification to deforestation. Sustainable practices are essential for preserving the country's natural resources.

8. Tourism Potential: Jordan's historical and natural wonders offer immense tourism potential. While the pandemic had a significant impact on the industry, the country continues to promote itself as a tourist destination.

9. Cultural Heritage: Jordan's rich cultural heritage is a source of national pride and a valuable asset. Preserving and promoting this heritage is both a challenge and an opportunity.

10. Renewable Energy: Jordan is making strides in adopting renewable energy sources like solar power. Harnessing its abundant sunlight has the potential to reduce reliance on fossil fuels.

11. Regional Cooperation: Jordan actively participates in regional organizations and initiatives. Strengthening ties with neighboring countries offers opportunities for economic cooperation and stability.

12. Diplomacy and Mediation: Jordan has a history of engaging in diplomatic efforts and mediating conflicts in the region. Its role as a peacemaker presents opportunities to contribute to regional stability.

13. Vision for the Future: Jordan's leadership has outlined a vision for the country's future, including economic reforms, technology advancements, and social development.

The challenges and opportunities facing Jordan are intertwined, reflecting the nation's resilience and adaptability. As Jordan navigates its path forward, it does so with a commitment to preserving its heritage, addressing its challenges, and seizing opportunities to build a brighter future. The journey is marked by a sense of determination, grounded in the understanding that, as history has shown, Jordan has the strength and vision to overcome adversity and flourish in a changing world.

Famous Jordanians: Icons and Influencers

In this chapter, we explore the lives and contributions of some famous Jordanians who have made a mark on the world stage. These individuals have excelled in various fields and have become icons and influencers, not only within Jordan but on a global scale. Let's take a closer look at their achievements and the impact they've had:

1. Queen Rania Al-Abdullah: Queen Rania is not only the queen consort of Jordan but also a prominent advocate for education, youth empowerment, and humanitarian causes. Her work has earned her recognition and respect internationally.

2. King Abdullah II: As the current monarch of Jordan, King Abdullah II plays a vital role in the country's stability and diplomacy. He has been a strong advocate for peace in the Middle East and has worked tirelessly to maintain Jordan's position as a regional peacemaker.

3. Princess Haya bint Hussein: Princess Haya is known for her humanitarian efforts and contributions to equestrian sports. She served as the president of the International Equestrian Federation (FEI) and has been involved in various charitable activities.

4. Nadia Murad: Although not originally from Jordan, Nadia Murad, a Yazidi human rights activist and Nobel Peace Prize laureate, has found refuge in the country. Her advocacy for the rights of women and minorities who have suffered under ISIS has garnered international attention.

5. Noura Al Kaabi: Noura Al Kaabi is a notable Emirati-Jordanian figure in the world of media and culture. She serves as the UAE's Minister of Culture and Youth, contributing to the promotion of arts and culture in the region.

6. Dr. Rana Dajani: Dr. Dajani is a respected scientist and educator known for her work in genetics and her commitment to improving education in Jordan. She founded "We Love Reading," a program dedicated to promoting a love for reading among children.

7. Marwan Juma: A successful entrepreneur and tech visionary, Marwan Juma has played a crucial role in advancing Jordan's information technology sector. He co-founded Oasis500, a leading accelerator for technology startups in the Middle East.

8. Ibrahim Nasrallah: An acclaimed Jordanian-Palestinian author, poet, and novelist, Nasrallah's literary works have received international recognition. He has been awarded prestigious literary prizes, contributing to Jordan's vibrant literary scene.

9. Luma Qadoumi: Luma Qadoumi is a contemporary visual artist known for her innovative and thought-provoking artworks. She has exhibited her creations worldwide, representing Jordan's thriving art scene.

10. Hani Al-Mulki: Hani Al-Mulki is a distinguished economist and politician who served as Jordan's Prime

Minister. His contributions to economic policy and governance have had a lasting impact on the country.

11. Amer Al-Madani: A prominent lawyer and human rights activist, Amer Al-Madani has been a vocal advocate for legal reform and social justice in Jordan.

12. Ayman Safadi: Ayman Safadi is a diplomat and politician who has held key positions in the Jordanian government and has been a significant figure in international diplomacy, particularly in addressing regional conflicts.

These famous Jordanians have made significant contributions to their country and the world, leaving a lasting legacy of leadership, creativity, and advocacy. Their stories serve as inspirations, reflecting the diversity of talent and potential within Jordan's borders.

Epilogue

As we bring our journey through the diverse and fascinating land of Jordan to a close, it's worth reflecting on the many facets of this remarkable country that we've explored. From its rich history, vibrant culture, and stunning landscapes to its warm hospitality and promising future, Jordan has proven to be a nation of immense depth and significance.

Throughout this book, we've traced Jordan's history, from its ancient civilizations to its modern monarchy. We've marveled at the architectural wonders of Petra, the majestic landscapes of Wadi Rum, and the surreal waters of the Dead Sea. We've savored the flavors of traditional Jordanian cuisine, from mouthwatering dishes to delectable desserts.

We've also delved into the intricacies of Jordanian culture, from the diverse population to the nomadic traditions of the Bedouin. We've explored the language, artistry, music, and religious tolerance that define this nation. We've celebrated its festivals and learned about its educational system.

In examining Jordan's economy and its role in the region, we've witnessed its growth and potential as a hub of stability. We've gained insights into its monarchy and the legacy of its royal family.

We've explored the challenges and opportunities that lie ahead for Jordan, emphasizing the importance of preserving its heritage and promoting sustainability. Finally, we've acknowledged the famous Jordanians who have left their mark on the world stage.

As we conclude our journey, it's clear that Jordan is a nation of resilience, diversity, and enduring beauty. Its people have shown a commitment to progress, peace, and prosperity. Whether you're planning a visit, seeking to understand this captivating country better, or simply appreciating the tapestry of cultures that make up our world, Jordan will continue to leave an indelible impression.

In closing, we hope this book has served as a valuable guide to Jordan, offering insights into its past, present, and future. May your own journey to Jordan, whether in person or through the pages of this book, be filled with discovery, wonder, and appreciation for all that this remarkable nation has to offer. Jordan's story is far from over, and its pages continue to be written by the people who call it home and the visitors who are inspired by its magic.

Printed in Great Britain
by Amazon

42936030R00069